MAINSTRE

DAYS LIKE THESE

THE EDUCATION OF A RACING LOVER

JAMIE REID

MAINSTREAM
PUBLISHING

EDINBURGH AND LONDON

This edition, 2004

First published in Great Britain in 2003 by
MAINSTREAM PUBLISHING (EDINBURGH) LTD
7 Albany Street
Edinburgh EH1 3UG

ISBN 1 84018 895 2

Reprinted, 2004

A catalogue record for this book is available from the British Library

Typeset in Van Dijck and Janson and Bastard

Printed in Great Britain by
Cox & Wyman Ltd

'I write to preserve things I have seen, thought, felt,
both for myself and for others,
though I feel my primary responsibility is to the experience
itself, which I am trying to keep from oblivion
for its own sake.'
– Philip Larkin

For my mother and father

CONTENTS

CHAPTER ONE   9
CHAPTER TWO   20
CHAPTER THREE   26
CHAPTER FOUR   37
CHAPTER FIVE   44
CHAPTER SIX   55
CHAPTER SEVEN   62
CHAPTER EIGHT   68
CHAPTER NINE   78
CHAPTER TEN   89
CHAPTER ELEVEN   98
CHAPTER TWELVE   111
CHAPTER THIRTEEN   123
CHAPTER FOURTEEN   135
CHAPTER FIFTEEN   146
CHAPTER SIXTEEN   156
CHAPTER SEVENTEEN   165
CHAPTER EIGHTEEN   176
CHAPTER NINETEEN   187
CHAPTER TWENTY   196
CHAPTER TWENTY-ONE   208
POSTSCRIPT   220

CHAPTER ONE

And so here we go again. Another year, another Cheltenham Festival. The opening day, Tuesday, 12 March 2002. Horses and riders, bookies and punters and the old familiar smells, of crushed grass and cigar smoke, of champagne bubbles, beer and newsprint. Along with that very particular and contemporary Cheltenham flavour: the stench of fast food – onions and hot dogs, burgers and hot beef sandwiches – drifting across the course like the smoke from a toxic barbecue.

High up in a box in the main stand the big players come and go. Movers and shakers in the gambling and currency markets. Irish and London accents predominating. The hospitality, it seems, in never-ending supply. Wine. Champagne. Canapés. Lunch. Roulades of salmon and medallions of beef. And the view from the balcony is breathtaking. Yet high up in a box you miss something too. You are shielded from the sheer and overwhelming intensity of the Festival. The sound of the horses, the rush of air and the collective longing of 50,000 racegoers jammed together on the lawn, all nervously fingering their betting slips. We've waited two long years for this day to arrive. An entire Festival, a whole season of expectation, lost to the foot-and-mouth epidemic 12 months before, creating an almost intolerable demand for Cheltenham action and excitement. And now it's only a few minutes away.

An electric surge of adrenalin flows around the track as the runners in the Supreme Novices Hurdle canter down towards the start. I can feel my heart beating faster. A knot in my stomach. Mouth dry. My money, my judgement, my fluctuating confidence, all are riding on the favourite. The eight-year-old mare Like A Butterfly. Owned by J.P. McManus. Trained on the Curragh by Christy Roche. And ridden by Charlie Swan. A trio of protagonists I'd back against anyone at Cheltenham.

They've had this contest in mind for their horse ever since April 2001, when she won Ireland's most valuable Bumper, or National Hunt flat race, at Leopardstown, by seven lengths. Some observers immediately labelled her a stayer. They said she'd be likely to lack the speed to win the two-mile Supreme Novices and according to the statistics she'd be too old to do it anyway. Only Roche and J.P. didn't see it that way. As the trainer had breathlessly and conspiratorially intoned the previous summer, 'She would have all the stamina in the world . . . and all the speed in the world.'

Christy Roche. A former seven-times Irish champion jockey on the flat. An Epsom Derby-winning rider. A man who had worked for Paddy Prendergast and David O'Brien, for Jim Bolger and Aidan O'Brien. A trainer, a breeder, a horse dealer. A self-confessed lover of a bet. Four feet eleven inches of natural horsemanship and native cunning.

And J.P. The Sundance Kid. The ex-bookie turned multi-millionaire gambler and Manchester United shareholder. So very charming and generous and soft spoken on the outside. And so very sharp and crafty underneath.

And Charlie Swan. Straw hair, a smile full of teeth and ingenuous good humour concealing one of the best judges of pace in the weighing-room. Three times a Champion Hurdle-winning jockey on Istabraq. Nobody rides Cheltenham's hurdle racetrack better than Charlie does.

These men are winners and they know their likely top Cheltenham prospects months in advance. Everything will be done to get those horses to the post fit and well with their best performances still to come. And if they do run, having made the expected improvement from October to March, their odds on the day will be a fraction of the early-season prices.

Which is why in October 2001 I took 10–1 about Like A Butterfly with a naive English bookmaker. £100 each way. And from that point on I've been watching her odds contract by the week. On 18 November 2001 she makes her hurdling debut at Navan. With Charlie up. The 6–4 favourite in a field of 28. An indication of how highly she's regarded. She wins, eased down by eight lengths. She's cut from 10–1 to 8–1 for Cheltenham. I stick on another £100 each way.

On 2 December 2001, she lines up for the Royal Bond Hurdle at Fairyhouse. A Grade One race worth over £37,000 to the winner. She takes it by four lengths from Edward O'Grady's Sacundai. A starting price of 4–7. In Cork and Dublin they cut her from 8–1 to 9–2 for the Supreme Novices. In England she's still 6–1. I stick on another £200. Win only.

On 28 December, it's the Stillorgan Hurdle over two and a half miles at the Leopardstown Christmas meeting. She beats Pietro Vanucci by half a length at odds of 2–7. She has to be ridden from the last. 'My horses have been a bit sick,' says Roche. There's speculation that her Festival target is in doubt – though I'll wager it was never in doubt to J.P. and Christy.

On 10 February 2002, she's back at Leopardstown for the Grade Two Deloitte and Touche Novices Hurdle. A £23,000 race with ten runners and a quality field too. She's in front four out. She gradually winds up the pressure and goes away to win by five lengths. Sacundai is second again. Adamant Approach, who'd been victorious in the valuable Pierse Handicap, is third. And a certain Beef Or Salmon finishes in the rear.

Past evidence shows that this February race is a serious Cheltenham pointer and I continue backing her at 4–1 and 7–2. Come the day I'm in pretty deep. In the paddock she looks strong and well and ready to roll but she's done all her racing on soft or heavy ground. Will the going at the Festival be too firm for her? That's my biggest worry but the punters around me don't think so. Especially not the Irish, who've backed her in to 7–4 on the track and for whom she represents that fatally enticing notion, the 'banker' of the meeting.

The Scottish bookmaker Freddie Williams thinks she can be beaten. He's laid J.P. a hundred grand at 15–8 and he's been on to the internet betting exchange, Betfair, trying to lay off his liabilities. He's got eighty thousand on at 2–1 or better. He's quite a character is Freddie. The former factory worker who bought out a Scottish mineral water business and ended up a millionaire. Freddie Williams. The man with the number-two pitch in Tattersalls at Cheltenham. A shrewd and fearless bookie, a friend of the serious punters and a gentleman. Not afraid to play or pay. So much so that the other bookies joke that he must have an awful lot of bottles of mineral water hidden away up there in Ayrshire. A man who has had a triple heart-bypass operation, and whose idea of healthy recreation is to take on J.P. McManus. Not just in March either, but regularly throughout the winter. A man who loves jump racing and who is clearly not afraid to go out on his shield. Here's to him . . . but I hope he loses this one.

Some form-book judges and statistical experts don't fancy Like A Butterfly either. The views of some of them are always worthy of respect. Yet there are one or two who will put you off everything including life. Desk-bound and devoid of passion, they seem incapable of functioning away from their speed figures and their private handicap ratings. They're entitled to their opinions of course. Everyone who bets on a racehorse is playing for his- or herself. Yet everyone who gambles has something in common too, and it's not just a hunger for the money. If your £40 or £400 on a 7–4 shot is the last £40 or £400 you've got in the world, you're as big a punter as Freddie Williams and J.P. McManus. And at Cheltenham there is some sense of a shared enterprise – calculated and reckless, hard-headed and bacchanalian – that unites punters and racegoers of otherwise wildly different backgrounds and financial circumstances. Go to a French or American racecourse and you'll be lucky to see the public cheer a winner they haven't backed themselves. Go to the Festival and you'll see it every year.

The starter's calling them in. My nerves tighten another notch and I can feel a tense ache behind the eyes. I take a quick look back at the bookies' boards. She's still a rock-hard 7–4 at the off. The money's down alright. The tapes rise and a great cheer goes up from the crowd. Celebratory, optimistic and, after last year, louder than ever.

Charlie is quickly away and right up there from the start. He's taking no chances. She's very fit. She'll stay the distance twice over. So keep her handy, he's thinking. Make plenty of use of her and don't let her get boxed in behind the pack.

An outsider falls at the second hurdle leaving the mare in front. She's got a high cruising speed and the pace is strong. They race out down the far side and she's joined by the champion jockey Tony McCoy on Martin Pipe's Westender. A course winner the previous November and the 6–1 second favourite. McCoy leads at the third and kicks on, Like A Butterfly following. Adamant Approach, well beaten by the mare at Leopardstown but trained by that other great Cheltenham specialist Willie Mullins and ridden by the brilliant Ruby Walsh, is also close up. So too is 'Storming' Norman Williamson on Donnie Hasset's Native Scout.

Five from home. A.P. McCoy and Charlie Swan. The pace increasing. The pressure's on. They hit the top of the hill and swing left-handed for the start of the long run back. The downhill hurdle and it's Like A Butterfly who lands in front. Adamant Approach right up with her; In Contrast and Richard Johnson closing and Westender suddenly under pressure.

They make the final left-handed turn. One flight to jump, and the cry goes up. The same cry that accompanied Istabraq's Champion Hurdle challenges in 1998, 1999 and 2000. 'Go on, Charlie. Go on, my son.' The noise ripped out of my lungs. Throat seared. Swan and Walsh coming to the last and it's Adamant Approach who looks marginally in front and going the strongest. But then he falls. Ruby's blue jacket with the blue and white checks suddenly disappearing as if the horse had been shot from under him. And yes, oh yes. Am I lucky or what? It's the mare, it's the J.P. McManus colours, back in front on the rails – but it's not over yet. McCoy has got Westender running again and the most fearsome sight in jump racing, Tony McCoy in full cry, is storming up the hill after Charlie. This mare though, she's something. She's brave and she's tough and she won't give in. Head down, neck out, inching, inching home. The punters cheering. The horses engulfed by a wall of sound. She makes it. By a neck.

Charlie waves a finger at the crowd. His boyish face jubilant on the big screen in front of the stands. I'm still swaying. Head spinning, heart pounding. I love these moments. I love them with my life.

It's roughly 27 hours later. Pushing 5.30 on Wednesday afternoon, 13 March 2002. Overcast with a strong wind and the temperature falling. And just one race to go on the second day of the Festival. The Grade One Champion Bumper over two miles and half a furlong.

For some of us there is no race anywhere and certainly no betting race quite like the Cheltenham Bumper. It brings with it a ravenous, feral urge not just to gamble but to follow the money, the clues, the scent and to hark to the sound of dogs barking.

A Bumper, or National Hunt flat race, is the traditional closing contest of every afternoon of Irish jump racing – and many in Britain too – from Leopardstown to Thurles and from Fairyhouse to Gowran Park. It's usually run over two miles. There are no hurdles or fences and the contestants are not ex-flat racers, but young jumping-bred horses who may have run in a point-to-point but are now taking their first official steps on a route that might lead to the very top. Or may just be a one-off gamble on a January day. A farmer and permit holder – meaning an amateur trainer – landing a touch and then selling on his exciting discovery to the men with white Mercs and flapping cheque books. Representatives of Mr J.P. McManus, Mr David

Johnson or Mrs Sue Magnier. Who might in turn send the horse to be trained by Christy Roche or Martin Pipe. By Eddie O'Grady or Jonjo O'Neill.

The Cheltenham Bumper being a championship race, the entrants have to have run at least once, though none of them must have been out more than three times. Amongst the contenders this year is the 3–1 chance Alexander Milennium, trained by Willie Mullins (successful a remarkable four times in the Bumper's ten-year history) and a 20-length winner of his only run to date at Leopardstown on 27 December.

Then there's Back In Front, trained by O'Grady. The winner of a Bumper at Cheltenham the previous November, proven on good ground, with Charlie on board and trading at 12–1. There's his stable companion Pizarro, a handsome chestnut, victorious at Naas on 24 February, trading at 14–1 and ridden by the stylish young flat-racing jockey Jamie Spencer, a regular work rider for O'Grady in the winter and not afraid to take on his more robust National Hunt colleagues.

There's Iris's Gift from Jonjo O'Neill's Gloucestershire yard, unbeaten in three races, already a Cheltenham course winner and on offer at 20–1. And then there's his stable companion, the six-year-old Rhinestone Cowboy. Owned by Sue Magnier, ridden by 'Storming' Norman Williamson and described in awed tones by connections of the owner and trainer as 'perhaps the most exciting horse ever to run in a Bumper in England'.

Rhinestone Cowboy. A son of the top National Hunt stallion Be My Native, and a former lead horse for Aidan O'Brien's two year olds on the gallops at Ballydoyle. A creature quick enough to set the tempo for such priceless commodities as the lightning-fast Johannesburg, the champion juvenile of 2001 and a winner at the Breeders' Cup meeting in New York. If such a horse can translate his flat-racing quality to the jumps then surely one of Cheltenham's glittering prizes will be his.

We'd only been permitted one previous glimpse of the Cowboy on the track, in a Bumper at Ascot on Saturday, 16 February. Where J.P. McManus just happened to be in attendance, and strolled up to the Victor Chandler pitch on the rails and asked the famous bookmaking firm what odds they might offer him about Jonjo's in the last. Victor's men, playing their hand as cannily as J.P., asked what price he was looking for. Around 5–1 would be fair, he suggested. They smiled and shook their heads and offered him 5–2. He said that was no good to him and continued along the rails in search of a more gullible bookie. He found a few too, and once his money had spoken at 3–1 and 5–2 the odds plunged to 6–4. Rhinestone Cowboy won by seven lengths pulling up. So much for 5–1 being fair.

Of course to be the ultimate Festival talking horse, in the Bumper of all races, is to be part of a rather chequered Cheltenham tradition. In 1992 there was a colossal tip for an animal called Tiananmen Square, also owned by Sue Magnier, who was sent off the 6–4 favourite and whose defeat by the better-ridden Montelado was a disaster for the big hitters. Twelve months later a horse called Heist galloped so hard that in the words of the irrepressible ex-trainer Mick O'Toole 'he looked like a bicycle frame', was turned over at odds of 9–4.

In 1998 Joe Mac, trained by Christy Roche, owned by J.P. and named after one of his sporting heroes, Joe Mackenna of Limerick's 1973 champion All Ireland hurling team, was the medium of another frenzied gamble. He too was a 6–4 favourite but he was turned over by the Willie Mullins runner Alexander Banquet.

The following winter Roche and J.P. were said to have another Bumper ace in their pack. Youlneverwalkalone (the name chosen to tease the Irish racecourse commentator Des Scahill, a devoted Manchester United fan) was a 'steering job' at Leopardstown over Christmas and the hot ticket in the ante-post Festival market. Only then he had 'a little setback' and never made it on to the plane.

They were the bookies' friends. Yet what we believed in 2002 – what I believed ardently – was that Rhinestone Cowboy was in the mould of something different. The genuine Cheltenham 'good thing' exemplified by the Mullins-trained Wither or

Which, the 15–8 Bumper hero in 1996, and Florida Pearl, effortless winner for the same stable in 1997.

Rhinestone Cowboy opened up in the ring at 5–2. Earlier in the day, hungover and fatally emboldened, I'd decided to play up my Like A Butterfly profits and had placed £2,000 on his elegant nose. Five grand to come. Maybe.

Cheltenham winnings are, well . . . Cheltenham winnings. Of course you try and keep a bit for that pressing bill or tax demand. Or, more joyously, for presents for children, wives and lovers, and drinks and largesse for friends, but mostly you spend it there and then on the track or in the bar and restaurant that night, or you leave it behind with the bookies. You can't take it with you, as Victor Chandler says mischievously. Too right. It's like winning at a casino or card game, where it's almost bad form to walk away too soon with your readies. It's as if some magnetic force compels you to stay, to play some more, to give a bit back.

The race wasn't off until 5.45 p.m. but, superstition being my regular companion, I'd left the racetrack nearly half an hour before. I'm mainly an ante-post punter. I like sticking to the classics or Group races on the flat and the Graded races over jumps: races with a history and a discernible pattern. Races where it's possible to beat the market days, weeks, even months in advance. Races where you know everything's trying and where certain top-drawer trainers and jockeys – Roche, Charlie, O'Grady; Aidan O'Brien and Sir Michael Stoute on the flat – have a ruthlessly focused strategy and a dependable strike rate not matched by other less capable outfits. Yet whenever I've stepped out of character and had a larger than usual bet at Cheltenham, be it in cash or on credit, and been there to watch it run . . . it's lost. Fallen maybe. Or been brought down. Or just had no luck in running.

So by 5.30, as Jonjo and Norman, the Magniers in their hats and long coats and all the other sleekly groomed owners assemble in the paddock, I've already dashed off into Cheltenham town. Taking a cab from the rank up by the horseboxes near the Evesham Road roundabout, getting out near the Odeon cinema and disappearing into a local branch of Ladbrokes on Winchcombe Street. A place of decent anonymity. Betting-shop punters packed in wall to wall. Faces glued to the big TV screens. Racing lovers who couldn't afford a badge or ticket for the day. Punters who've left the track early and headed into town. Locals who can be found in the same betting office six days a week whether it's Cheltenham or Hexham. And the once-a-year curious, their work over for the day. Like a friendly faced cashier from the local Halifax branch two doors down, usually to be seen framed by adverts for 'low-cost personal loans' (Hah!), mortgages, credit cards and high-interest accounts. Now squeezed between a fruit machine and a pillar, his copy of the *Gloucestershire Echo* turned open at the racing page. Eyes trained on the action and no doubt his heart beating just that little bit faster. Like mine.

Away they go. In the unnaturally bright television light. It's much gloomier on the course as six o' clock approaches. I watch over heads, around shoulders and behind hands and for the first half of the race I see more of Cleeve Hill in the background than I do of the horses at its foot. Then suddenly they're racing down the hill with just over three-quarters of a mile to run. Thisthatandtother, with Timmy Murphy riding, is in the lead. Back In Front with Charlie is close up on the inside. Alexander Milennium has been pulled up but Rhinestone Cowboy, travelling smoothly on the bridle as expected, is beginning to make ground from the rear. So too is Pizarro.

Three furlongs out, the bottom of the hill and it's Charlie now in front and going strongly. The Cowboy is tracking him on his outside but Pizarro and the angelic-looking Spencer are throwing down a powerful challenge on the inner. 'Come on, Norman,' I'm muttering under my breath. 'Let him down. Press the button. Let him go.'

They've got a furlong to run and they're starting up the hill. Rhinestone Cowboy comes through to lead. As he does so Pizarro hangs to the right, pushing Williamson towards the rail. The Cowboy rallies and runs on but then Pizarro bumps him again within yards of the winning post. Pizarro crosses the line first but surely it's inconceivable he can keep the race. There has to be a Stewards' Enquiry and probably an objection too from Norman Williamson. Rhinestone Cowboy has to be adjudged the winner.

In the crowded shop we wait. They replay the finish two or three times and watching it again I'd back my judgement, based on everything I know about racing, that the first and second places will be reversed. An amusement machine pays out. Dogs' shows and results go on interminably and then there's a review of the day. Finally, after a near 20-minute wait, comes the Stewards' decision. The result stands. And I've done my money.

My head light, stomach empty, I push out through the door onto the street. It's getting dark outside and an army of retreating racegoers are already flowing back into the town. I look across the road at an electricity showroom and at another building society, both of them closed and locked up for the night. The usual fumes belch out from Burger King on the High Street, and I feel as if I've been sitting in the grill tray.

Other punters are walking past me, heading towards the pubs, bars and hotels. One of them pauses to considerately throw his rolled-up *Racing Post* into a dustbin. I'm tempted to do the same but instead I buy an evening paper with tomorrow's declared runners.

Outside a Yates's Wine Lodge I hail a taxi. 'Now then, sir,' says the driver enthusiastically. 'Was it a good day at the races?'

'Not exactly,' I reply.

How did I get here?

CHAPTER TWO

It began really with my grandmother, Marie Elizabeth Tanner. She was a tall and strikingly handsome woman with long, auburn hair and a piercing eye. It was sometimes suggested that she was perhaps a little eccentric in some of her habits and tastes, though few people were bold enough to tell her so directly. She preferred the company of men to women and sometimes cruelly preferred that of her three sons to her youngest child, a daughter and my mother.

Born in 1877 when Queen Victoria still had more than 20 years of her reign left to run, this similarly indestructible personality died 2 weeks short of her 90th birthday. And almost every day of her adult life, from the age of 18 to that penultimate week in hospital, she had a bet on a racehorse. It was her example and inspiration that first led me to appreciate what a beautiful and uplifting spectacle horse racing can be. She taught me that a racecourse was one of those places in British culture, one of the very few in her lifetime, where non-conformity was not always a crime. And where one could expect to savour something of the full gamut of human behaviour in all of its pungency and colour, and out of reach of the propriety and convention of the everyday world.

I have learned many other lessons about horse racing since.

I have learned that win or lose, there are few things I lov
so wholeheartedly as skiving around on a racetrack in th
company of friends. I have learned about betting and about
what seems to me to be the inherent impossibility of winning
at it consistently and I have discovered that for some people,
myself and my grandmother included, it seems inherently
impossible not to try.

When I was a child and growing up in the village of Leigh in
west Kent, Mrs Tanner was living on the edges of nearby
Edenbridge in a red-brick Victorian house called The Thorns. It
was surrounded by a rambling garden complete with orchard
and shrubbery and with open fields beyond. At the bottom of the
garden, one of my uncles – a complete lunatic who went around
everywhere in his Old Alleynian cricket blazer and a brown trilby
hat – kept chickens. There were a large number of cats too, some
of whom stalked the chickens enthusiastically while others
hunted rats in and out of the granary.

A quiet lane ran past the front gate of the house and beyond
that ran the equally quiet railway line from Victoria to
Edenbridge Town, Eridge, Groombridge and Tunbridge Wells
West. Primroses and violets grew on the embankment in
springtime and small fires started there regularly in summer, set
off by hot sparks from the tenders of the passing trains.

My earliest memories of my grandmother are of the
excitement of visiting her by train with my mother in the late
1950s, when I would have been about four or five years old. I
remember the smoke and the steam and the grit in the eyes as
the huge engines arrived in Leigh's minute station. The heavy
doors slamming and the porter waving his stiff green flag. The
carriages were still the old, bottle-green rolling stock of
Southern Region with their comfortable buttoned upholstery
and pictures of salubrious south-coast watering holes – Cooden,
Hythe, St Leonards-on-Sea – up beneath the luggage rack.

The return journey always carried with it an extra element of
tension and fear. There was an unusually high step up from the
platform at Edenbridge top station and as we sat shivering in the

...ter afternoons, breathing in the smell of the ...cretly worry about whether I would be able to ...ep up successfully. Or whether I might slip and ...ugh the gap onto the track. Or whether the train ...noving before we were safely inside.

...iologist might make something of those fears as a precu... .r of the worries and anxieties of adult life, be it as shiftless punter or model citizen. There's no doubt that an element of apprehension and fear was a distinctive theme of those Edenbridge visits. Even aged four I could sense that Mrs Tanner was a formidable old lady and her house was forbidding too with its dimly lit halls and corridors and thunderously flushing lavatories with their heavy wooden seats and iron chains. I found it all rather dark and fearful while being drawn simultaneously to the frightening places.

In fine weather I might be outside in the garden watching the cats chase each other round the shrubbery, but more often than not I would be wandering alone through the cobwebbed rooms of the house. Marvelling at the jumbled and haphazard collection of antiques and other objects. Many of them were old and dusty. Some of them were beautiful and bizarre but all of them were richly evocative to a small boy's imagination.

There was a great bronze bust of the Emperor Justinian. An African spear. A looming black marble eagle which I later came to think of as 'The Maltese Falcon'. A smaller black marble elephant with shining white ivory tusks. Cupboards full of yellowing old newspapers, pre-1914 postcards and magazines. Complete Spode and Crown Derby tea and dinner services. A crackling Churchillian wireless set. A wind-up gramophone along with stacks of records from His Master's Voice. Sagging Edwardian chairs and sofas. And a long, black, polished-oak dining-table that could seat more than 20 when all the leaves were out at Christmas and came complete with a set of very grand leather-backed dining-room chairs.

The imposing yet ramshackle nature of my grandmother's possessions seemed all of a piece with her eccentric and up and down progress in life. From sometimes perilous Victorian childhood to promising Edwardian marriage. From 1920s and '30s comfort and prosperity to the eventual bankruptcy and death of my grandfather. Who was clearly a spiritual forebear of mine, albeit one denied joint ownership of my grandmother's things by a marriage contract drawn up by her own wise stepfather in 1907.

There was nothing about the atmosphere of The Thorns that was remotely comparable to the neat, secure and ordered world of my parents' post-war detached house in Leigh. And I was always quite glad when it was time to leave Edenbridge and go home again, but I was also intrigued by what I might find when I next went back.

Grandma had a scullery and kitchen with a big walk-in larder and an old, stone sink with bronze taps. Along with numerous pots of China tea, Mrs Tanner loved drinking Guinness and there were always open bottles and half-full glasses of stout standing around on the kitchen table. Enabling me to take surreptitious sips when no one was looking.

Pinned up to the kitchen wall, conveniently close to the telephone, were assorted racing and bookmaking calendars along with the private and business numbers of leading representatives of firms like Heathorns, Ladbrokes and Hills. More Turf publications would be lying around on the table and chairs, mingling with the most recent editions of the specialist racing papers such as the *Sporting Life* and *Chronicle*.

By 1959 I'd seen a bit of racing on television. Mainly coverage from places like Goodwood on the BBC and Plumpton and Folkestone on Southern. Where dear old John Rickman would, with unfailing courtesy, raise his trilby hat and wish us all 'Good afternoon' at the start of proceedings. I liked what I'd seen and wanted to know more and said as much. So one winter's day in 1960, my grandmother conducted me into the narrow, dark and high-ceilinged room that connected the kitchen and scullery on one side with the main part of the house on the other.

Up against the wall was a rich-brown mahogany chest of drawers and inside those drawers was a veritable racing library. Form book after form book. Year after year. Season after season. Jumping and flat. Their myriad details of results, odds, owners, trainers, jockeys, sires, breeders, courses, distances and going just about encapsulated the entire history of the British Turf from Edward VII's final Derby win with Minoru in 1909 to the era of Parthia, Petite Etoile and St Paddy 40 years later. These books were to be my guide, my key into a secret garden of infinite fascination and I lay around reading them for hours. First in that dark room in Edenbridge and then later on at home after my grandmother, surprised but delighted at my interest, had given me most of them to keep.

I read about Crepello and Pinza and Tulyar and Hyperion. I read about Brown Jack and The Tetrarch. I read about Cottage Rake and Golden Miller, Easter Hero and Sir Ken. I read about the Aga Khan and Prince Aly Khan, about Fred Darling and Noel Murless and Jack Jarvis and Walter Nightingall: and about the Lords Derby and Roseberry and Sir Victor Sassoon. I read about Lester and Sir Gordon and Steve Donoghue and Doug Smith and Bill Rickaby and Charlie Smirke. And I read about the French jockeys too, about men with names such as Roger Poincelet and George Thiboeuf, about Jacques Doyasbère and Jean Deforge.

I learned about betting returns and market moves and about odds and fractions and SPs. I learned about the names and distances of all the major races and about their date in the racing calendar. And I learned about the racecourses, great and small, including some now long-forgotten and closed-down venues such as Woore, Wye and Buckfastleigh. Rothbury, Bogside and Hurst Park.

Poring over these faded but irreplaceable Turf histories I began to ask questions about their owner's history too and from what she told me then and from the many details filled in later by my mother, I was able to build up some kind of picture of the remarkable racing-mad Mrs Tanner. A woman who, I afterwards felt, was at least one part Miss Havisham in *Great Expectations*. And a woman whose life seemed to have been characterised by a quintessentially Dickensian mixture of comedy and eccentricity, darkness and light.

CHAPTER THREE

Marie Elisabeth, or Marizia as she was christened, was born in London in 1877. Her mother, Frances Emily Hallett – the daughter of Henry Hallett, a Wiltshire sheep farmer – had eloped at the age of 16 with one Henryk Stapfelkamp, a Dutch artist and engraver. Stapfelkamp was tall and slim and auburn-haired. He was clever and talented with it, but also considered to be habitually lazy by his family.

Frances Emily was barely 17 when Marizia was born. Another daughter, Louise Cordelia, followed in 1879 and then in 1881 there was a boy, Henri, who died of tuberculosis when he was ten years old. The family went to live in two rooms in Portman Square, an address now renowned in the racing world as being the London headquarters of the Jockey Club.

Frances Emily found work sewing the ornamental braid on to the tunics of new officers in the Household Cavalry. My grandmother would sometimes be sent on errands to the silk wholesalers' shops in Little Britain. And she remembered hurrying back through the darkening streets in the autumn of 1888, clutching the parcels of material that her mother had ordered and hearing the newsboys standing on the street corners shouting, 'Another Ripper. Another Ripper.'

Henryk Stapfelkamp engraved the pillars of the Church of St

James in Spanish Place and worked for the distinguished Victorian painter Sir Lawrence Alma-Tadema. But his life continued to be characterised by a fatal, if charming, indolence. And in 1889, when Marie was 12, her father ran off suddenly to Paris with a French chambermaid, and was never heard of again.

The Dutch grandparents, horrified by their son's desertion of his young wife and children, came over from Holland to help out and for a while Henryk's mother Marianna ran a stewed eels shop in Drury Lane, next door to the Royal Opera House. Without her intercession, my grandmother and her little sister and brother would very probably have ended up in the workhouse.

Henry Hallett had moved up to London too on the death of his wife Cordelia, who was said to have been a tartar by my grandmother and who had effectively severed all communication with Frances Emily after her elopement. With the money that Henry brought, along with the help of the Dutch in-laws and the income from her work, Frances Emily was able to make a better life for them all.

The three children were sent to the French Lycée Henri Quatre in Marylebone and Marie in particular proved a quick learner with an especial talent for languages, music and verse speaking. Her best friend at school was herself the daughter of a French émigré, who owned an alimentation and charcuterie shop in Charlotte Street, and Marie spoke French fluently throughout her life, extending her enthusiasm to backing nearly every French-trained favourite in an English classic race.

When Henry Hallett died in 1891 my great-grandmother decided to take in a lodger and the new man turned out to be almost as colourful a card as Henryk Stapfelkamp. Alexander Braun, another émigré, was a Hungarian cabinet-maker with a penchant for Viennese dancing. It soon became clear that he had a penchant for Frances Emily too and that the attraction was mutual. Mr Braun began escorting Mrs Stapfelkamp to a series of dances and musical evenings around London, their love affair progressing happily over the waltzes, polkas and gavottes.

It may've been something of a relief to get out of the Portman Square lodgings as great-grandma's brother William Hallett had recently come to stay. William had been blighted by a tragic romance and he carried his love letters around with him in a carpet bag. Each evening he would take them out and read them while lying on the sofa and weeping prodigiously. He was also in the habit of putting on his overcoat and hat and taking his umbrella with him when he went upstairs to bed at night.

Mr Braun's business did well and in 1893 – by which time he and Frances Emily were living together as man and wife, although they were never formally married – they all moved to Shepherdess Walk off the City Road. Marie and Louise kept house there in the mornings while in the afternoons Marie, who'd left school at 16, went as a companion to the wife of the painter Sir Frederick Leighton. Within a few years, though, the family was on the move once again, this time out of London altogether.

Mr Braun had decided to try his hand at running a pub and in 1895 he became the landlord of The Bull on Kelvedon Common in what in those days was still a green and leafy corner of Essex. The Bull was not far from one or two routes to Newmarket and enjoyed its fair share of the racing trade and it was around this time that my grandmother started to take a serious interest in the Turf. Perhaps mindful of her father's treatment of her mother, she was not yet ready to take a serious interest in marrying or settling down, and for that period continued to lead something of an independent life until well into the next century.

Marie had taken on a lot of the bookkeeping and accounting at The Bull and would have quite liked to have run her own business. 1905 found her working as a hotel manageress in Virginia Water in Surrey. It was by all accounts a lively place. Parties of Edwardian swells used to visit regularly from London and Grandma enjoyed the atmosphere. For all her hard-headedness she was always susceptible to a bit of charming and good-looking male company and it was in the grounds of this riverside pub that she first set eyes on the man she would eventually marry. He came riding out one Sunday morning, looking impossibly dashing and theatrical, on the black mare that was his regular mount in the Life Guards.

Frank Gillard Tanner was a man of great sartorial splendour who loved to do everything in style. He was born in 1881, the eldest son of Frank Popham Tanner, a master butcher from Street in Somerset and later from Redcliffe Hill in Bristol. If it was from his West Country childhood that Frank acquired his love of horses and riding, then it was probably from his mother, Clarissa Gillard, that he inherited his enthusiasm for clothes. Clarissa, who came from County Westmeath in Southern Ireland, loved to dress well and spent a considerable sum of money on her wardrobe. She sometimes found it politic to conceal from her husband precisely how much. Should she want some new kid gloves, for example, she would buy six pairs but all of them in white. Wearing a different pair each day, she would be able to keep up appearances while convincing Mr Tanner that she'd been wearing the same pair all week.

Young Frank, it seems, was cut from similar cloth. Like a true Edwardian, he believed that there was an appropriate costume for every occasion and he turned to them all with gusto. It began as a child with the choirboy's robes he wore each Sunday in the Church of St Mary Redcliffe in Bristol and continued with the various sporting colours he was awarded at Clifton College. Then in his adult life there were his cavalryman's uniforms and evening dress, his cricket and tennis whites, his astrakhan-collar coats and his spats and suits and Norfolk jackets. Vain maybe, extravagant no doubt, but looking good and looking appropriately dressed, no matter the cost, was one of Frank Tanner's greatest pleasures in life.

Clarissa Gillard adored her son and was always prepared to help and humour him if she could. At the age of 18 he'd joined the Household Cavalry. By 1906 he'd grown tired of it but his commission still had two years left to run. He managed to persuade his parents not only to buy him out but also to set him up financially so that he could propose to Marizia.

The couple were married at St Mary Redcliffe in the April of 1907. An eldest son, Francis, was born in the December of 1908 and two more boys followed, one in 1910 and another in 1913. My mother Paula wasn't born until 1922. By which time Marie was nearly 45. And I think that if Grandma was sometimes unkind to her youngest child and more dismissive of her than she was of her three athletic sons then it was partly out of irritation at finding herself 'burdened' with the responsibilities of motherhood again at a relatively mature age. Frank, by contrast, was gentle and affectionate with his daughter, who worshipped his every move.

I've never been exactly sure what Frank Tanner did for the best part of his working life. Or where the money came from – or what black deed or catastrophic deal it was that led to his eventual downfall. At one point he was buying carpets for Whiteleys in Queensway. Then he was the owner of a jewellery shop in Wardour Street and going into business with Gordon Selfridge, before parting company with the other man – a bit like changing your bets or your horses at the last minute – just as Selfridge made it into the big time. For all the unhappy ending, Frank and Marie were able to live in some style together for the best part of 30 years, most of them spent in the house my mother grew up in on the edges of Streatham Common in south London. Now a rather different neighbourhood to the prosperously middle-class outpost that it resembled during the first three decades of the century.

Number 44 Braxted Park was a double-fronted Edwardian house in a peaceful, suburban street. There was a large back garden where my grandmother kept a greenhouse for her flowering cactus plants and her geraniums and there was a separate tradesman's entrance in the rear garden wall. The local butcher used to deliver by horseback, the meat orders arrayed on a board across his saddle.

My mother says there was a great feeling of comfort and solidity about Braxted Park. The various rooms all had their own different shades and moods whether they were full and vibrating with the laughter and conversation of her parents' guests or quiet and sleepy on a summer's afternoon.

The entrance hall led on one side to a long dining-room, which, after the fashion of the time, was kept half-dark during the day. The old oak dining-table that would end up in Edenbridge stood in the centre of the room while the sideboard was not only where breakfast dishes were displayed, but also acted as a permanent home for the collection of gold and silver cups and other trophies that my grandfather had won for athletics both at school and in the cavalry.

The Tanners entertained regularly and my mother remembers quantities of ice being brought up from the fishmonger to help with the preservation of the food. The larger the dinner parties, the more complicated the preparations would be, and the more noise and chinking of glasses my mother would hear from her bedroom upstairs. She would slip down daringly to finish off the dregs in the wine glasses, much as I would sip my grandmother's Guinness more than 30 years later.

There were two pianos at Number 44. One of them was kept in the dining-room but the light in there was generally so poor that my mother used to joke that you could barely see the keys. The other piano was in the drawing-room, which was across the other side of the hall. It was there that my grandparents would adjourn with their guests after dinner. Frank and Marie both loved to sing. He would launch into sterling renditions of 'Sparkling Eyes' and 'The Road To Mandalay' with Marie accompanying him on the piano. She had a beautiful voice and would sing mainly French songs and operatic arias.

My grandmother's singing teacher, an Italian lady by the name of Madame Fumigali, came to the house once a week. My mother remembers her as large and fierce and always dressed in black, including exotic black capes and feathered hats. Her stately approach along Braxted Park resembled some imperious galleon cutting a path through the Mediterranean waves. Madame Fumigali's visits would climax with tea and special cakes served on the best Crown Derby tea service. My mother witnessed all of these occasions, although she was well drilled to be seen and not heard and to speak only when spoken to.

Everyone in the family had music lessons: Mrs Tanner saw to that. My mother was taught singing and the piano by the Miss Boltons, a pair of spinster sisters who lived close by. She had elocution and deportment lessons too, being compelled to walk around a room with a book on her head so as to learn how to stand up straight and walk with her shoulders back.

Her three brothers had their piano lessons with another deserving matron by the name of Miss Evestaff, who, for some reason best known to my grandmother, attended upon them at the house at half past seven in the mornings. Here she would find them still half-asleep and struggling to get into the striped trousers, black jackets and stiff collars of their prep school uniforms. Perhaps not surprisingly, a talent for music played little part in their adult lives.

The boys were all destined to go on to Dulwich College, where, like their father, they excelled at sport in general and cricket in particular but otherwise achieved little of distinction. In their earliest years they were enrolled as day boys at Cheltonia College in nearby Ambleside Avenue.

The headmaster, a small, thin, bespectacled man called Mr Thomas, was very much under the thumb of his formidable and buxom wife Mrs Thomas, who required not only the unfortunate boarders but also her husband to take a cold bath each morning. And also to consume large quantities of the cod-liver oil that was placed on the dining-room tables at mealtimes. My grandmother was scornful of these arrangements, believing that heartier food and an end to cold showers would not only do wonders for the well-being of the boys but also improve the conjugal relationship of the Thomases.

It was entirely characteristic of Mrs Tanner to be contemptuous of convention the one minute and then cheerfully reactionary the next. She had no time whatsoever for Mr Thomas and his type but she still wouldn't have dreamed of sending her sons to anything other than a fee-paying school. And while she prided herself on being as sharp and quick-witted as any bookie or businessman, she still restricted her only daughter's education to a genteel convent.

Frank and Marie went out almost as often as they entertained at home. Frank was an accomplished after-dinner speaker and much in demand. His easy-going charm and skill at making connections had resulted in him becoming chairman of the Buyers Provident Association and intriguingly, especially in view of how little they did to help him when the wheels came off, he was also Grand Master of the Lion and Lamb Masonic Lodge – an institution cordially loathed by my grandmother.

The Tanners went to Masonic functions together. They also went to the opera and the Café Royal. Mrs Tanner's evening clothes, from Madame Marks in Knightsbridge, included a long, pale green, satin dress worn with a white fox cape, including the head and tail and a wine-coloured, velvet dress with chiffon flounces at the back like a mermaid. My mother also remembers an evening jacket lined with variegated satin and finished with a collar of black bear.

When Gordon Selfridge threw a lavish fancy dress ball in 1926, Grandma went as Marguerite from *Faust*. Her auburn hair untied and loose over her shoulders. It seems she had no shortage of male admirers, Selfridge included, but none of them were more ardent or more constant in their attentions than her bookmaker. Charles Allen.

There were no betting shops in Britain in the 1920s or at least no legalised off-course offices. Punters who were in a position to do so had accounts with the credit bookie of their choice and it was the south Londoner Charlie Allen who saw the best of my grandmother's business.

Mr Allen, so the stories go, was a most stylish operator. All dove-grey suits, pearl-grey cufflinks and snap-brim trilby hats. If Grandma was racing in person she'd be able to stroll over to Charles Allen and strike a bet with him at his pitch on the rails. Otherwise she conducted all her wagering by telephone, sensibly waiting until her husband was away up in town or at work.

Frank and Marie's bedroom at Braxted Park was a handsomely furnished room with two enormous wardrobes and a beautiful hand-carved dressing-table that had been given to the couple as a wedding present by Mr Braun in 1907. Next door to the bedroom was my grandfather's study, a rather more ambiguous room where he would sometimes slope off with friends to smoke cigars, drink whisky and soda, tell risqué stories and pass around photographs of half-naked women.

It was in the study that the telephone was kept and each morning my grandmother would ensconce herself there with the racing pages and duly send her pounds and shillings down the line to the bookies. Sometimes Charles Allen called at the house in person. Grandpa would be out then, naturally, and the bookmaker, always immaculate and always polite, would be shown up to the first-floor study. From where my mother, should she be at home and not at school (much to Mrs Tanner's irritation), would hear the sounds of laughter and conversation.

I think that in her prime, Grandma won more often than she lost. But when she lost heavily and couldn't pay her bills in full, she was in the habit of offering Mr Allen various pieces of jewellery or items from her collection of Meissen china as an alternative to cash. I believe these trophies were always accepted more than willingly, although there was clearly a subtext to their relationship whereby the settlement sometimes took another form as well.

When the bookie left an hour or so later he was always the soul of discretion. A courteous raising of the hat to Grandma, followed by a wink, a 'Cheerio, dearie' and maybe half a crown left on the table in the hall for my mother. Who later that day would slip into the study when no one was looking, pick up the telephone and say: 'This is Mrs Marie Tanner speaking. I'd like to talk to Mr Charles Allen. I want five pounds to win on Brown Jack in the three o' clock at Ascot.'

My mother believes that Mrs Tanner's special relationship with her bookmaker lasted at least until the late 1930s when the financial disaster that overwhelmed Frank eroded Marie's ability to gamble on her old scale. While my grandmother may have necessarily kept the details of her private liaison from the outside world, her love affair with the Turf was open and unapologetic. Like most punters she developed an attachment to certain horses she would back over and over again and that grand old pre-war stayer Brown Jack was one of her favourites. Others were the 1933 Derby winner Hyperion and the great steeplechaser Golden Miller, who won the Cheltenham Gold Cup an astonishing five times running between 1932 and 1936. And many years later, when I was a child, she would talk rapturously about the brilliant grey filly Petite Etoile who was ridden by Lester Piggott, trained by Noel Murless and owned by the Aly Khan.

Petite Etoile won the 1959 1,000 Guineas and Oaks and then the following season defeated the previous year's Derby winner Parthia in Epsom's Coronation Cup. Petite Etoile's odds, reflecting her ability, were never particularly generous and as a gambling medium, Grandma preferred the old-fashioned handicaps like the Great Jubilee at Kempton Park and the City and Suburban and Great Metropolitan at the Epsom spring meeting. These were races that had been in their heyday at the turn of the century when Mrs Tanner was a young woman. Even in the late 1950s they still provided a strong ante-post betting market and plenty of coups and touches to get excited about.

I think that Epsom was probably her favourite racecourse (I was wheeled across the Downs in my pram in 1955), but she could be equally enthusiastic about Kempton, Lingfield and Ally Pally (Alexandra Park). She also had a soft spot for Brighton, another passion that has been passed on in full to her grandson. The family often took a house down on the south coast during August and a large party would be invited (including a totally barking Dulwich schoolmaster by the name of Eddie Reade). My mother remembers Frank and Marie going racing in style every day that it was on.

By the 1930s, Grandma's own mother, Frances Emily, was living at Lancing with the still sprightly Mr Braun, who'd bought the auction rooms at Portslade. The debonair Hungarian, who was said to swim in the Channel in all seasons and who never suffered a day's illness in his life, died in Brighton in 1943. He was tucked up in the arms of one of his several mistresses when her flat took a direct hit from a flying bomb. Frances Emily's view of the couple's demise was, alas, not charitable.

Frank Tanner's business career had been shot down in flames six years before, the cause of his sudden betrayal in some ways as mysterious as the origins of his success. In 1932, fortunes apparently still booming, the Tanners had moved from Streatham to Chelsham Lodge, described by my mother as 'a lovely old rambling house' near Warlingham in Surrey. Sadly demolished in the 1960s, it came with two large fields, an orchard, stables and tennis court and to my mother it represented the very acme of pre-war happiness and security.

After Frank's fall in 1937 the house had to go (and Grandmother's savings went with it), though thanks to that fortunate marriage contract drawn up 30 years before, the furnishings and contents remained unsold, all of them accompanying the Tanners down to Edenbridge, then still a pretty Kent village surrounded by hop gardens and farms. Frank, who continued to take a few stiff whiskies and a Monte Christo cigar with his breakfast bacon and eggs, died there of a heart attack in 1944.

When I started visiting Grandma some 14 years later, the memories of Frank and Marie's lifetime together were everywhere in the ether of The Thorns. But the ruined old lady who presided over those memories was still very much alive. And still every defiant inch a punter.

CHAPTER FOUR

A love of betting and racing and a willingness to risk more than you can afford on the outcome of a six-furlong handicap may have been something I inherited from my grandmother, but it was by no means typical of my kind but cautious parents.

My mother Paula would, I think, have secretly rather loved to inhabit the world of the racetrack. To enjoy a little luxury and style to travel in comfort and to drink champagne after every success. Unfortunately life wasn't easy and such hedonistic options rarely presented themselves. And even if they had, to indulge in them recklessly, as I have done, would've been wholly out of character for my father.

Alex Reid was a gentle, decent man and handsome too in his youth. He was devoted to his wife and children and he believed in hard work and early rising, living within your means and putting a little by for a rainy day. His appetite for danger and risk had, I think, been satiated brutally in 1943. Yet he never attempted to impose a safe or conventional career on me. Far from it. And, as I eventually realised, he dedicated the greater part of his working life to making sure I would one day be able to enjoy precisely the kind of freedoms and opportunities that he had been denied.

At its best, Leigh, and the surrounding green-belt countryside of south-east England, was a happy and comfortable place in which to grow up. Village life, not yet decimated by speeding traffic and property speculation, had retained something of its pre-war hinterland of pubs, shops and schools along with its local bus and rail services. And the surrounding landscape of orchards and hop gardens, woods and fields was everything that the Garden of England sounds like and ought to be. Alas, though, life was not all some cheerful paradigm of innocence and fun à la *The Darling Buds of May*, and I remember the prevailing mood of the late 1950s as being more one of grim disapproval than genial joy.

My own parents may have been gentle, unthreatening figures, but adults from the outside world were continually exhorting one to stick within rigidly proscribed behavioural guidelines and the penalties for disobedience were high. This was still the era of corporal and capital punishment (Ruth Ellis went to the gallows the year after I was born), and backstreet abortion. Homosexuality was an imprisonable offence. Single mothers were often ostracised by their communities and teenagers were constantly being reviled for their deplorable lack of respect for their elders and betters. 'I fought the war for your sort' was a line we heard long before Richard Vernon delivered it to John Lennon in *A Hard Day's Night*.

You can forget all that Soho brasserie retro chic too. There were no style-file icons or gleaming chromium-plated hubcaps in Tonbridge High Street circa 1959. America. That was the land of wealth and glamour and infinite possibility. But the Britain of *Two Way Family Favourites* and *The Black and White Minstrel Show* was as far removed from any notions of cool as Kent was from California. And in the south-east in particular it seemed as if much of the old 1930s and '40s snobbery and class consciousness had persisted and survived with a grim but unconquerable spirit.

Villages like Leigh were a mixture of old houses, new houses and council houses and interrelations between the various inhabitants often felt like the inspired *Frost Report* sketch on class. The one featuring the tall John Cleese as a caricature of the upper classes, the shorter Ronnie Barker as a representative of the middle class and the even shorter Ronnie Corbett as the archetypal 'worker' in overalls and a flat cap. Like the sketch, residents of the village's older and bigger houses looked down on those in the newer houses who in turn were encouraged to look up to their betters while looking down on the families in the council houses. Who were expected to look up to everyone.

My mother may have grown up with the kind of people who lived in the bigger houses and my father may've gone up to London each day on the 7:41. He may've worn a suit and tie and a brown trilby hat and looked quietly distinguished with his well-trimmed moustache. He may almost have looked like a stockbroker but unfortunately and fatally he was not a stockbroker. He was a carpet salesman and he worked in a shop. And according to the prevailing social code of the occupants of the bigger houses that, well, that just wouldn't do.

Educational status was equally important in determining relationships. My grandmother may've abhorred and lamented the fact, but I was going not to the local prep school, Hilden Grange, and then on to Tonbridge public school but to the village primary instead. Where as one of only two or three children of the supposed middle classes, I was pretty much thrown to the wolves. Discovering at an early age what it was like to be a loner in a crowded playground and soon working out that a few well-chosen words, fluently delivered and targeted at an appropriately sensitive or vulnerable subject, can wind an opponent every bit as effectively as a punch to the solar plexus. And that comedy, satire and sedition, be it administered with a rapier or a machete, can be an invaluable weapon in life. Even if one is sometimes too inclined to get one's retaliation in first.

There were all kinds of pressures on us at primary school but none were more intense than the pressure to get on, to do well, to grasp the educational lifeline by passing the Eleven Plus and going on to become not 'a typical Secondary Modern lout' (as one of the village's matrons witheringly described them) but a grammar school boy. Who might in turn pass more and harder exams and continue onward and upward into the First World. We might never quite make it into the company of those who enjoyed perfect BBC vowels and had drinks with cherries in before lunch, but we would at least put some distance between ourselves and the lower classes. Becoming not – whisper it softly – Teddy Boys or 'hooligans' in winklepicker shoes but conforming to the acceptable ideal of duffel-coat-wearing, trad-jazz-listening, voluntary-serving, Christian Conservative youth.

Perhaps it's an aspect of everyone's experience that when we look back on our childhood we remember certain details, objects and images with greater clarity and sharper definition than we associate with more blurred episodes from adult life. And that it's only to be expected that if I shut my eyes I can still feel the brush of my father's moustache, the touch of his suit and the smell of his pipe tobacco as, thinking me asleep, he would lean over to kiss me goodnight after some late-returning winter train ride back from London.

Perhaps it's only to be expected too that I can still vividly recall the power and beauty of the steam-pulled boat trains that used to rush through Tonbridge station on their way to and from Victoria and the coast. And picture the giant revolving Kiora orange in Fortes café on Tonbridge High Street. And the indomitable range of women's underwear that was always on display in the window of Frank East's shop opposite.

The teachers, policemen, sportsmen and politicians of that era also seem – through the selective lens of memory – to have been bigger, stronger and more authoritative than their slippery and ersatz contemporary equivalents. But there was a bleak and oppressive side to life too. A sense of national inhibition that didn't begin to crumble until the aftermath of Labour's General Election victory in the autumn of 1964.

Some recent cinematic versions of British life 30 and 40 years ago tell you more about the lifestyle fantasies of the 1980s and '90s than they do about what it was actually like to be alive at that time. The great black and white movies of the early 1960s, like

A Kind of Loving, Saturday Night and Sunday Morning and *The Loneliness of the Long Distance Runner,* were far more realistic.

I remember an awful lot of greyness about between 1958 and 1963. When, as John Osborne remarked, you could attract outraged looks just by walking down a provincial High Street in a yellow cardigan. Tonbridge High Street emptied totally within half an hour of six o' clock closing time. Things livened up briefly around 7.30 and then again three hours later as the pubs called last orders and the cinema's main feature ended. And then, with the sound of the national anthem still ringing in their ears, a few groups of restless 'youths' and bee-hived girls would eye each other up outside the chip shop or in the bus shelters as they waited for the last, dangerously late, services to the outlying corners of the town.

Sunday was the worst day of all. Our spirits battened down as Osborne's much-loathed church bells tolled over streets and cafés as locked up and deserted as the bleakest one-horse town in the salt flats of Utah. Nobody could be nostalgic for that.

I remember too the waiting and queuing and satisfied complaining of English life. Shortages were still felt keenly even 15 years or more after the end of the war. Macmillan may've told us that we'd never had it so good but couples like my parents still enjoyed precious few luxuries or opportunities for travel and escape. Financial worry and the unspoken longing for a less restrictive life was often etched on their anxious faces. And I could hear it in their voices too and in whispered conversations that took place late at night when they thought I was lying asleep upstairs in my bed.

I had longings of my own. For adventure, glamour and romance. Beyond the field at the top of our garden was a cutting through which ran the tracks of the Tonbridge to Redhill, Guildford and Reading railway. The hourly rumbling of the little two- or three-coach passenger services (the same train that conveyed us up to Grandma in Edenbridge) and the clatter of the occasional freight were always regarded as a soothing background accompaniment rather than as something noisy or polluting.

On dry summer days sparks from the locomotive's tender might alight on the grass in the field and start a blaze. And then the fire brigade would be summoned, red engines hurtling towards the action from the gap behind Moon's garage. And there would be a temporary truce among all the children of the village as old houses, new houses and council houses united together to enjoy the spectacle.

Local passenger services and long, lumbering goods trains weren't the only rail traffic through Leigh. Twice a week the line became the route for an altogether more exotic Pullman express service called the Birkenhead, which ran from Dover Marine to Merseyside and in the years before I started at school and then in the holidays, the days when this special train was due were precious ones.

As the appointed hour drew near I would race across the field towards the cutting and then stand by the fence, gazing down in rapt fascination as the beautiful chocolate and cream carriages rolled by. I could see the pink-shaded lamps on the dining-car tables and often just catch a glimpse of the starched white napery and all the gleaming spoons, forks and knives. The people sitting at those tables, sipping from glasses, cigarette in hand or casually ordering their lunch, seemed to me to be impossibly confident, stylish and grand. Their world surely was the epitome of luxury and involved none of the making do and going without to which my parents had grown accustomed. Now that, I thought, is the life for me.

By the early 1960s, my father's old firm, Hamptons, which used to stand on the corner of Trafalgar Square and Northumberland Avenue had, sadly, closed down. Its quietly traditional methods and absence of self-promotion had proved no match for the newer, brasher world of hire purchase and Cyril Lord. My father, weary of the grind of daily commuting, came to work in Tunbridge Wells instead, managing the carpet department of a large store called Chiesmans.

Once the typical county town big shop, Chiesmans was already destined for the status of a sort of superannuated Grace

Brothers from *Are You Being Served?* Its founder Stuart Chiesman was a former Lord Lieutenant of Kent whose daughter Penny became the first Mrs Colin Cowdrey. The family's grasp of their empire, which extended throughout the South East from Canterbury to Hove, was a tenuous one and before long ownership had passed from them to the House of Fraser and then onto the Army and Navy stores. By the time my father retired in 1979 the windows, once pristine and smart, were awash with garish cut-price stickers and details of sensational new promotions. And by 1996 the whole building had been split up and sold off. But by then my father was ten years dead.

There used to be a top-floor restaurant at Chiesmans, a quaintly old-fashioned setting for coffee, cakes and currant buns. I often used to drop in on my father at work when I was down from university during the vacations and he would invariably take me up to the restaurant and show me off to his colleagues with quiet pride. I owe him so much. For his unfailing kindness, patience and support. And for all the long years of nine-hour days and five-and-a-half-day weeks (with just three weeks holiday a year) that he endured to help subsidise my start in life.

He never once put pressure on me to conform to the same narrow nine-to-five path that he had been bullied into. He always said that if I could manage to survive by doing the things I loved, then I should do so unashamedly and try not to be sunk by the consequences. I don't know what he'd have thought of the mess I eventually made of things, but I do know that his love was unconditional. And without end.

CHAPTER FIVE

My grandmother had planted the seed of betting and racing in my imagination and my parents, partly without realising it, had encouraged me to dream of an expansive life. Until I was old enough to go racing in person, though, it was the power of the televisual image and the mesmerising effect of one man's voice that ensured my passion would thrive.

One March morning in 1961 I came down to breakfast with an unusually swollen neck and face. It didn't hurt in the least but my mother was sufficiently alarmed to take me to the doctor. Our local GP, a tweedy and moustachioed ex-RAF type who tended to pinch small boys rather more than was necessary, cheerfully proclaimed that I had mumps. And he said that I would have to stay off school for the next two weeks. I couldn't believe what I was hearing. This surely was an act of God. An entirely unexpected and unlooked-for holiday. Two misery-free weeks in which to idle, daydream and play.

On the Monday morning of the second week of my fortnight's quarantine my grandmother rang. There was, she said, something rather special on television over the next few days. Two hours every afternoon devoted exclusively to horse racing from Cheltenham. The home, so my grandmother told me, of steeplechasing. Of the National Hunt Festival. I was lucky I was free. I should watch it. So I did watch. And it's no exaggeration to say that the impression it made on me has pretty much dictated the pattern of my entire life.

In those days our television set was still a fairly recent acquisition and it spent much of its time on a table in the corner, as if it might not be entirely trustworthy or respectable. When you wanted to watch something it would be wheeled out into the centre of the room but you couldn't just switch on and sit back. You had to give it a few minutes to 'warm up', sometimes administering the odd bang or kick to get the picture working.

I had previously associated daytime television with nothing more exciting than *Rag, Tag and Bobtail* and *The Woodentops*, but from March 1961 whenever the TV was switched on as early as 2 p.m. on a weekday afternoon it could mean only one thing. Horse racing.

I shall never forget that first Cheltenham Festival and it's a tribute to the power of the medium that the old black and white television images should've made such a powerful impact on my imagination. The weather that week was cold but dry and the visual spectacle of Prestbury Park, bathed in early spring sunshine, was a stunning one. Never before had I seen a racecourse on such a scale. With such a wide and galloping track, with so many gradients, with such a long downhill run to the home turn and with an equally long uphill run to the finish. And always in the background you could see the majestic sweep of fields and hills and Cotswold sky. This was nothing like Kempton Park or Stratford or even Newbury, all of which were sometimes featured on *Grandstand*. And it was absolutely nothing like dear old Plumpton or Catterick Bridge, which still cropped up regularly on ITV.

Even to a not quite seven year old the racing was self-evidently intensely competitive. Some contests had fields of twenty or more, others small but select bands of seven, eight or nine. There were four televised races each day and they seemed to feature champions, characters and so-near-but-so-far heroic failures in wave after wave. I still remember the names of those horses as if they were the most recent winner, or losing favourite, I backed at Chepstow only yesterday afternoon. There were Fortria and Pas Seul and Saffron Tartan. Another Flash, Albergo and Farmer's Boy. There were Eborneezer, Moss Bank and Richard of Bordeaux.

I remember the jockeys too. The Irishmen Bobby Beasley and Pat Taaffe. Bill Rees, who rode for the Queen Mother. Stan Mellor. Terry Biddlecombe. And most memorably of all Fred Winter. He became the first of my weighing-room heroes, winning both the Champion Hurdle on Eborneezer and the Gold Cup on Saffron Tartan in the same week. A feat only rarely achieved in the history of Cheltenham races and one still as rightly and highly prized today as it was 42 years ago.

I knew nothing about Winter the man except that he appeared to be modest, brave and courageous. A fit role model for those clean-cut days. And it was clear even to my novice eyes that he was a jockey who could inspire, drive and cajole a horse to quite astonishing effect. Winning races that others would have accepted as lost. Getting back up on the line when all chance of victory seemed to have gone. And launching his mounts up the Cheltenham hill with a great competitor's irresistible will to win.

What a character too, albeit a contrasting one to his stable jockey, was the trainer Captain Ryan Price who saddled Eborneezer to win the Champion. Here was a man whose style and demeanour appeared to have been modelled directly on Captain Hook. There was the trilby hat at a permanently rakish angle, the binoculars slung over one shoulder, the cigarette in hand and an expression at once foxy and imperious. This Captain was a man to be reckoned with. A man, what's more, who was winning the Champion Hurdle for the third time. Impressing on me early on in life that some people have what it takes to win at the highest grade and can do so again and again. Whereas others, no matter how successful or well regarded they may be elsewhere, can never quite make it to the top. 'Yes. But can you really imagine them training a Cheltenham Festival winner?' is the question I still find myself asking every time some new fresh-faced hopeful, some new Henry or Nigel, is being touted as the coming man.

My experience of March 1961 was not only about inspirational horses and their charismatic trainers and riders. Nor simply of the far-flung racecourse and its stirring backdrop. What made that first Cheltenham Festival for me, and what was to make every other Cheltenham and every other televised racing scenario for years to come, was the matchless commentary of Sir Peter O'Sullevan.

Like all the truly great sports broadcasters – like Arlott and Benaud on cricket, Maskell on tennis, Longhurst on golf – O'Sullevan combined a deep and profound love of and knowledge of his subject with a fluent and imaginative grasp of language. That inimitable and distinctive voice, with its rich timbre and mellifluous tone, was classic and classy but never affected or excluding. O'Sullevan's commentaries patronised no one and included everyone from the wealthiest Jockey Club grandee to the simplest armchair punter. He was one of the first broadcasters to democratise a sport in this way, but he was also a rigorous professional. And a man who understood that television is primarily a visual medium and that the essence of a successful transmission is not about head-to-head shots of bloke-ish presenters blathering away by the paddock rails. It's about the quality and smoothness of the visual images with the commentary as a background accompaniment.

To make the most of this medium, words should be used sparingly but to telling effect. In keeping with that principle, O'Sullevan's courteous but shy and fundamentally private personality infused his work, but always to its advantage and never the other way around. He was never a man to just gabble names frantically or to cheapen round the edges. His restraint as much as his grasp of high drama underlined that if you wanted to get close to understanding the beauty and magic of horse racing you mustn't spread it too thin or the outcome would be merely banal. For the big moments to count there had to be rationing and you couldn't start drumming up spurious excitement about routine races on uneventful afternoons.

Neither would you ever go to an O'Sullevan commentary for nudge-nudge, wink-wink asides to fellow members of the commentary team or for affected braying or a knowing smirk. One brashly opinionated sportswriter tried to put the boot in after a few audible mistakes were discerned during a 1990s Grand National broadcast. The target of the abuse would admit that by his very high standards there may have been a few lapses at that point in his career that would've been unimaginable even a decade earlier. Yet even a below-par O'Sullevan would never sound as arch or bored as his technically perfect but rather mannered Channel 4 rival Graham Goode, who outside of the very biggest races tended to come on like a shuttle pilot with British Midland. Going through the motions of welcoming the passengers aboard for the umpteenth Brussels or Belfast flight of the day.

O'Sullevan could not possibly know the result of a horse race in advance any more than those of us watching and listening with him, but what he did do, and what communicated to me so powerfully from the age of seven onwards, was unfold his commentaries like a story. An enthrallingly classical narrative with a beginning, middle and end. A story rich in drama and brimming with emotion and suspense. And a story with its own decisive moments of victory and defeat, triumph and despair.

I think what I also sensed as long ago as 1961 was that something about the very nature of Cheltenham racecourse enhanced and enriched every story set there. That long opening run up past the stands was the point at which everyone's hopes and expectations were still intact. Then would come the sweep down the far side and out into the country. Followed by the ascending uphill climb on the far side of the course. The top of the hill. The accelerating downhill chase. The left-handed turn into the straight. The final fence, as the noise of the crowd got louder and, for the horses, closer and more distracting and intense. And then that climactic uphill run to the death. These natural breaks and contours provided the perfect structure for O'Sullevan's commentaries. The paragraphs and chapter headings. Who would play their best cards when and how, and who would play their big cards first? Who would go too soon and tie up? Who would sit waiting in behind? Who would try and hold onto the lead from beginning to end? And who would come late and trump the pack?

When racehorses – and especially steeplechasers and hurdlers – remain sound and well and stay in training for season after season we get a chance to see in them patterns and characteristics as rich, diverse and unpredictable – though rarely as savage or treacherous – as we see in human beings. There are brave and courageous horses, lazy horses that deceive you and won't put it in and horses that never cry 'enough'. There are plain and plodding horses and horses that are arrogant and fast.

Peter O'Sullevan detests any kind of animal abuse and his work for equine charities has been well documented. His commentaries always respected courage and gameness in the four-legged competitors but he cherished flair and élan in the human protagonists too. And, as I began to understand as I got older and started to bet and race more seriously, he was a shrewd and consummate punter. And a man with the greatest respect for the professionals with the killer instinct. A big Irish gamble at Cheltenham. A crack French three year old on the flat. Lester Piggott and Yves St Martin. J.P. McManus and Vincent O'Brien. They were his type and it was for them that he reserved his highest praise. And if you knew what to look for and how to read the changing tones and inflections in his voice, you would find in his biggest commentaries that he always seemed to spot what the best were doing or were about to do, just before they did it.

Other aspects of the BBC's racing coverage grew stuffy and unimaginative over the years (although things have improved dramatically since Clare Balding replaced Julian Wilson as chief presenter in 1998). And there was a point when it seemed as if, with the exception of a few key meetings, the corporation's department heads and programme controllers had abandoned all pretence of covering racing on a regular and detailed basis.

These criticisms aside, does anyone really believe that Sky or Channel 4 could have persuaded up to 16 million people to stop what they were doing for an hour or more on a Saturday afternoon each spring and watch the Grand National on television? And would the viewers have turned on in anything like those numbers were it not for the man who was guiding them through the agony and the ecstasy of the closing stages?

O'Sullevan's Australian-born successor, J.A. 'Jim' McGrath, is a top-class commentator in every way but I know that for myself and for thousands of others like me, Sir Peter O'Sullevan was and always will be *the* voice of racing.

March 1961 culminated in the victory of Saffron Tartan, once a Festival-winning novice hurdler for Vincent O'Brien, in the Gold Cup. And after those three compelling days of drama and emotion were over I was left to experience for the first time the awful and crushing sense of anti-climax that overwhelms all steeplechasing lovers in the first few days and weeks after Cheltenham. A void filled initially only by the dismally inadequate spectacle of flat racing from Doncaster (or the Carholme at Lincoln as it was 42 years ago). And Grandma's Lincoln Handicap bets aside, we're talking about flat racing of unusually dire and threadbare quality.

Every year since 1961 I have continued to experience the two or three weeks after St Patrick's Day, or between the Festival and the Grand National, as the most barren period in the calendar, affecting not merely my feelings or outlook towards racing and sport but shading every nuance and aspect of daily life. It's a come-down every bit as severe as a child's depression in the first, bleak, new-term weeks of January. Though much like the child's enduring faith in the magic and possibility of Christmas, what gets me through is the sure knowledge that March will come round again. And that just like the early spring sunshine flowing into our home in Leigh all those years ago, the hope and fervour of the Cheltenham Festival will come round again too.

In the meantime, and hardly surprisingly, I soon grew to love the Grand National. Especially when I had a few bob each way with my grandmother on Nicolaus Silver, the grey horse trained by Fred Rimell and ridden by Bobby Beasley that won the 1961 running at 28–1. Come high summer I warmed to the bigger and better flat races, placing another few shillings each way on Pardao in the Derby. Trained by Major Dick Hern and ridden by Harry Carr, Pardao finished third at 13–2. The winner was a 66–1 outsider by the name of Psidium, who came fast and late to shade the French-trained Dicta Drake, owned by Madame Suzy Volterra. Peter O'Sullevan always and rightly listed the names of the owners along with their horses, jockeys and trainers.

Madame Volterra was one of a number of expensive-to-run women who had horses in that era. There was also Mrs Arpad Plesch and Countess Bathyanny and Madame Strassburger, who had owned the 1960 Derby favourite Angers. Then there were the waxed and silver-haired Frenchmen like François Dupre and Marcel Boussac, and the British ex-military types like Major Lionel B. Holliday, who owned Pardao. No owner of that period seemed more powerful and omniscient, though, than the financier Sir Victor Sassoon. He sensibly retained the services of Lester Piggott, who had quickly taken on the same status in my cast of heroes as Fred Winter had done over the jumps.

I thrilled to Lester's arrogance and flair and my favourite flat race of 1961 was his Ascot Gold Cup triumph on Pandofell, whom, regrettably, I was not allowed to support with hard cash. To this day I still love the big staying races on the flat. The Ascot Gold Cup. The Goodwood and Chester Cups. The Ebor Handicap and the Northumberland Plate. These were the events – with their length, their changing fortunes and ascending drama – that most closely resembled the pattern of a big steeplechase or hurdle race. And like the jumpers, the main contenders often came back again season after season. So that horses like Trelawney, who did the Ascot Stakes–Queen Alexandra Stakes double in both 1962 and 1963, soon became as special to me as the great pre-war Ascot specialist Brown Jack had been to my grandmother.

The favourite for Pandofell's Gold Cup had been a seemingly invincible French beast by the name of Puissant Chef and the 1961 Derby favourite had been another French colt called Moutiers. I soon began to realise that French horses on the flat posed the same regular and formidable challenge as the Irish did over fences. And of course, like cricketers from Australia and the West Indies, only seen in England once every four years, the overseas challengers enjoyed a far greater mystique and fascination back then because we saw them less often and knew much less about them.

There was next to no televised foreign racing in 1961 and frequent travel to the European mainland, let alone to America or the Far East, was still in its infancy. When it came to flat racing, French-trained horses seemed to be not only quicker but also more glamorous than our own. I shared the exhilaration when the top French three-year-old Right Royal V came over to Ascot for the 1961 King George VI, and Queen Elizabeth Stakes and routed the previous year's Derby winner St Paddy, who had Lester Piggott in the saddle. I could sense the charisma of these beautiful thoroughbreds and their cut-glass world and I wanted to know more about them but it was still only flat racing.

My big problem come March 1962 was not so much illness as the lack of it. You can only contract mumps once and, hard though I tried, I was unable to manifest even so much as a common cold or convincing 'bilious attack'. Let alone something really spectacular like chickenpox or measles, both of which arrived, infuriatingly, during race-free weeks in the school holidays. Ten years later my parents might have colluded in my unfortunate absence or at least turned a blind eye to my skiving off. It would've been a bit much to expect that kind of licence at the age of eight.

So of Fred Winter winning the 1962 Gold Cup on Mandarin (and riding the winner for the second successive year), I saw only snatched highlights on the six o' clock television news. And had to make do with similarly brief and tantalising glimpses of that year's Champion Hurdle in which the grey Anzio, trained by

Fulke Walwyn and ridden by Willie Robinson – two more names who were about to play resounding roles in my racing world – got up to beat the northern challenger Quelle Chance and the 1960 winner Another Flash.

Over the next 12 months my fascination with horse racing deepened and intensified and I think my understanding of its themes and patterns was already deepening too. At the start of each April and again in October, my grandmother sent me one of the smaller pocket form guides to the upcoming flat and jumping seasons. They may not have been on the scale of *Timeform's Racehorses of the Year*, but they were more than just racing for beginners and anyway I was learning fast. Each day I fell on my parents' *Daily Telegraph*, a paper that in a few years' time I would regard as risibly conservative, and read all the racing and sports pages avidly. And for all the Torygraph's solid right-wingery its sports pages, then as now, were among the best and most comprehensive of any broadsheet paper. John Lawrence (later Oaksey) aka Marlborough and Peter Scott aka Hotspur were, I suppose, my first regular tipsters along with the smaller-print form guide with all its intricate details about weight allowances and distances and somebody called 'Course Corr', whose identity was initially a mystery to me.

With my head full of names and figures I started staging my own racing games on the sitting-room floor. Toys, needless to say, were different in those days and with a little imagination my supply of cowboys, Indians and knights in armour could be transformed into the contestants in the Gold Cup or the National, the Hennessy or the King George. And by using toy building bricks, hedges and fences from old farm and zoo games and off-cuts of wood from the garage, I was able to make convincing scale models of Cheltenham and Liverpool right there on the carpet. I even wrote my own race cards, getting through sheaves of paper each week, and always using the names of real horses and trying to imagine the probable line-up for the big events to come. I supplied the names of the trainers and jockeys and sometimes the owners by each horse's colours along with a full form guide and betting show complete with my own selections.

I would then 'run' the races on the floor, moving each horse up and down around the track only partly according to whim and primarily according to how my intuition told me the race would unfold. I provided a commentary too, in my head if there was somebody else in the room, out loud if I was alone. And I was always Peter O'Sullevan. Daft obsession it may well have been, but horse racing was already giving me, quite literally, hours of pleasure. And I soon came to regard the Turf as a precious escape from the more wretched moments of growing up. Of which there were plenty. Most of them connected with school.

CHAPTER SIX

Leigh County Primary in 1959 was as sternly conventional as most Church of England village schools in late 1950s and early '60s Britain. We got six years' worth of religion, discipline and learning by rote as we shuffled in our Start Rite shoes towards the pitiless but unavoidable hurdle of the Eleven Plus. The system was expressly designed to weed out the 'backward' or less academically precocious children at an early age while launching a lucky few of us on the grammar school conveyor belt to the promised land.

The early years were the sheltered ones. Our infants teacher was a warm and bosomy Scottish woman who had young children of her own. She wore checked tweed skirts and tight jerseys with pearls and we could hear her stockings rustle when she crossed her legs while sitting reading us a story in front of the class.

Our time with Mrs Stirling, alas, passed all too quickly. The headmistress, Miss Nash, was a formidably strict, if generally fair, spinster in her early 60s but the real terror of our days was the teacher of the seven to nine year olds. A hairy-legged besom by the name of Miss Welch, who was a devout Christian convinced of the imperative need to crack down on the sinful tendencies of young children. Especially boys.

Good work was rewarded with stars and beans in a team jar. Bad work was punished mercilessly. And almost worse than any physical chastisement that Miss Welch might inflict was her capacity for brutal sarcasm, generally employed to expose our flaws in front of the rest of the class. There were days when children were being reduced to tears on an hourly basis and once their public cross-examination was complete they'd be sent back to their desks to sniffle in solitary misery.

Daunted by the prospect of imminent crucifixion, we chanted our multiplication tables and learned to write in a large, child-like hand. Chalk scraped relentlessly across the blackboard as we copied down grammatical and mathematical rules and memorised the names of the kings and queens of England. Miss Welch sometimes read to us out loud and they were good stories, too, like *The Lion, the Witch and the Wardrobe* and *The Borrowers*, but the books we had to use for our grammar and class reading lessons were mostly juvenile pre-war tales about Foxy Loxy and Chicken Licken. I preferred *Kidnapped* and *Treasure Island* and the latest newspaper reports from Lambourn and Newmarket.

We sang endless hymns and songs like 'Bobby Shafto' and 'The Raggle Taggle Gypsies-Oh' and we went for nature walks and kept wild flowers in jam jars on the window sill until they withered and died. We did some history and geography but very little science.

The first half-hour of each morning was devoted to a scripture lesson. Every autumn we were gripped by violent and retributive tales from the Old Testament. The story of Jacob and Esau and Jacob's Ladder was our favourite. At Christmas time we performed our allotted roles in the Nativity play. Miss Welch's favourite pupils were always Mary and Joseph. The rest of us had to make do with third sheep. The Easter term climaxed with the harrowing story of Christ's suffering on the Cross and even now I cannot hear the tune to the hymn 'There is a Green Hill Far Away' without shuddering.

The themes of pain, punishment, death and salvation criss-crossed our lives in sometimes bewildering ways. As we studied the Easter Story in April 1962, the papers and news bulletins were reporting on the story of James Hanratty, sentenced to death for the A6 murder. 'James Hanratty will be hanged tomorrow morning at Bedford jail,' declared a newsreader one balmy spring evening. The statement seemed all the more chilling given the quite ordinary and everyday events continuing in the background. The Shadows were still top of the hit parade with 'Wonderful Land'. Fred Winter was going to ride Kilmore for Ryan Price in the Grand National. Harold Macmillan had posed for the cameras in pinstriped trousers. And the following morning, while we were all eating our Rice Krispies and toast and Golden Shred, a man was going to have his neck broken in an English prison. With the full approval of the law.

'Don't worry,' adults reassured us. 'Only the wickedest people get hanged. And even then they don't feel anything. It's all over very quickly.' These sanguine words didn't fit with the muffled and sinister pictures of protesters gathered outside the prison walls and warders hammering the notice of death to the front gate. Who was the man in the dark suit slipping away into a taxi? And if it was wrong to kill, how could it be right to hang?

Some people were saying that Hanratty was innocent anyway and that he hadn't done it. Did that make him a sacrificial victim like Jesus Christ? And the Home Secretary and the other adults murderers like the Romans and the Pharisees? Could a hanged man be raised from the dead? Would a convicted murderer have the gift of eternal life? How could young children fit these confusing and disturbing messages into a dependable picture of right and wrong?

We all wanted to believe in the Resurrection while Miss Welch left us in no doubt whatsoever of the existence of Hell. And some children whispered that if you opened your eyes during the Lord's Prayer the Devil would see you and snatch you away.

Our classroom purgatory was defined by the typical primary-school smells. Paint, polish and farts mingling with the fumes of the coal-burning stove in the corner. In summertime we escaped outside to the village green to play rounders and netball and on winter afternoons we did music, movement and mime. Always in the same hall where we'd just eaten our school dinners. A shrill-voiced woman from the old Home Service would encourage us to be a piccolo or an oak tree swaying in the wind and at some point we'd end up face-down on the floor, our noses pressed into the lumps of mashed potato that had been spilled during lunch.

There were occasional moments of unforeseen joy, like the day when a conjuror visited the school or the morning Miss Nash informed us that Miss Welch had gone in to hospital for an unspecified operation and would be absent for at least three weeks. Most of the time, though, we were always frightened or worried about something or other. We were nervous of the punishments we might incur for infringing the rules. We were fearful of the larger consequences of educational failure and, when we were very young, we were frightened of the outside lavatories or 'backs' where the floor was always flooded with water and the doors wouldn't shut. And where anyone unfortunate enough to have to 'go' during playtime could expect to have the door barged in by some grinning tormentor. Or to be pelted with lumps of anthracite from the pile stacked up in the yard.

The terms dragged by, each more slow-moving than the last. You had to develop some kind of inner strength or fortitude to cope with the ritual humiliations. As I sat miserably at my desk waiting for the teacher to pronounce on my inadequate arithmetic, I would often slip into a kind of anaesthetised, private reverie. Wondering to myself who would triumph in the forthcoming King George VI Chase on Boxing Day or which of Ryan Price's runners would win the inaugural Schweppes Gold Trophy at Aintree. And reminding myself that however long each day in Miss Welch's company might seem, it would have to end eventually – and when it did, there would always be books to read and the racing pages, with their long-running cast of human and equine characters, to catch up on.

We may've been strictly disciplined in the classroom but outside in the playground and on the way to and from school there was no shortage of bullying and torture. Some among the generation of boys one form up from my own favoured a particularly insistent combination of physical and psychological intimidation. They had to be either confronted, dodged or rebutted on a daily basis. I could no sooner have shared with them my fascination with horse racing than I could've offered it up to Miss Welch as a substitute for my inaccurate fractions. They would've responded with incredulity and derision followed by the inevitable castigation of one who'd been foolish enough to stand out from the crowd. Their condemnation merely served to confirm me in my passion. And another reason I soon grew to love the world of the racecourse was that I appreciated the truth of what my grandmother had told me and understood that non-conformity was not always a crime in the racing milieu.

This may seem a paradoxical statement to the outside observer and, for sure, there are some aspects of horse racing that are thumpingly conventional from the formality of the royal enclosure at Ascot to the style and opinions of assorted stewards, trainers and racing officials. Yet the Turf is also a world in which I have consistently met just as many unconventional and non-conformist types from all backgrounds and classes. In other walks of life we might've set eyes on one another and taken in our different voices, appearances and styles of dress and imagined we had nothing whatsoever in common. But a racing person, especially a racing maverick, will always recognise another similarly free spirit and know that, uniforms aside, they have a shared and uninhibited enthusiasm for the beauty and vagaries of the track.

As an adult I like a good day's betting and racing to involve companionship and celebration, sociability and fun, but another of the great joys of the Turf is that as well as its extrovert pleasures it appeals just as strongly to the private, inner self. And you should never be afraid to follow your own instincts even if that cuts you adrift from the herd. I was often a solitary child myself but as long as I had books and the racing pages I was never a lonely one.

The icy weather of the infamous winter of 1963 wiped out all horse racing during January and February and by March I was longing for some sport. I was no more successful at manufacturing an illness than I had been the previous year but once again there were four televised races each day. And I found that if I got a lightning-fast break out of school at 3.30, I could run the return trip home, including a stiff uphill climb, in about six or seven minutes. This guaranteed me getting back in time to see at least the fourth race on the card, including the Gold Cup on the Thursday afternoon.

And there was no doubt that the star of the 1963 National Hunt meeting was the Gold Cup winner himself. Mill House. Or, as Peter O'Sullevan used to call him, the Big Horse, sending a shiver up my spine every time he said it. A magnificent great beast of an animal, he was. Owned, as O'Sullevan would also remind us, by Mr Bill Gollings. Trained by the master jumping trainer Fulke Walwyn. And ridden by an Irishman, G.W. 'Willie' Robinson.

I adored Mill House. With his relentless gallop and spectacular jumping, he seemed to me to be every inch the quintessential steeplechasing hero. I could tell from the tone in Peter O'Sullevan's voice that he thought so too. And no matter what came later, that 1963 Gold Cup run was a performance to take the breath away. It's almost unheard of for a six year old to win the jumping Blue Riband. Yet here was just such a horse, little more than a novice, routing the likes of the brave but luckless Fortria (who probably didn't really stay the three and a quarter miles any better than he had done the previous year), Frenchman's Cove, Duke of York, Caduval, Longtail and others. He was in front before the top of the hill second time around, more than three-quarters of a mile from home and from that point on he never let up, asserting his superiority gloriously by 12 lengths.

In just about every page of racing copy I could get my hands on from John Lawrence downwards, there seemed to be the same shared conviction, or perhaps it was just an intense hope, that English steeplechasing had a champion once again. A horse in the mould of the multiple-Gold Cup winner of the 1930s, Golden Miller. What might Mill House go on to achieve the following season? I could hardly wait for autumn to come round once again. We couldn't know then that whatever further and honourable distinction Mill House might attain, the high point of his racing career had already passed.

CHAPTER SEVEN

The essential flavour of the racing experience, no matter how it's sampled initially via television, can only really be tasted on the track. And while it's the performances of champions that light up the great days and the major stages, there are also smaller and more modest ways in which to defy puritanism and embrace the joyous, belt-loosening world of the Turf.

By 1963 I was beginning to get a taste of that intoxicating experience first-hand and my education had begun not at Cheltenham or Ascot but at the annual meeting of the Old Surrey and Burstow point-to-point, which took place each May in the fields behind my grandmother's house in Edenbridge.

Our family outings to the races were always conducted in the company of my parents' great friends Margaret and Gilbert Butcher, who lived at Penshurst. Margaret, a farmer's daughter from Charcott near Chiddingstone, was a fabulously attractive woman with a full figure and a dark, rather Spanish or Mediterranean air. Along with her humour and her vibrant personality, she emanated a tangible air of relaxed sexuality and seemed to me to be at once both sophisticated and yet earthy in the most alluring way. Margaret was an unfailingly loyal friend to both myself and my parents. She was also splendidly indifferent to convention and it's no exaggeration to say that her inspirational example did much to sustain me through the more miserable phases of adolescent life.

Gilbert Butcher, who was born in Chiddingstone, had left school at 15 to become a carpenter. By the late 1950s he was the owner of his own thriving building business which specialised in a standard of generations-old skill and craftsmanship not readily associated with some rival firms. Gilbert was a busy, laughing man with a shock of thick, black curly hair. He loved life and he loved racing and gambling in particular. Like my grandmother, he would occasionally let me have bets on his accounts, thus ensuring that on visits to the likes of Edenbridge, Ightham and Charing, I would not simply have to wager in cash on the amateur-ridden hunter chasers. I could be sure of having parallel investments on the Whitbread Gold Cup or the 2,000 Guineas that same afternoon.

Journeying to the races is a bit like the delicious contemplation of good food or sex. The anticipation is all part of the fun. I've been racing by helicopter, train and private plane. I've been chauffeur-driven in a white Mercedes. I've walked there and I've walked back. But no racing journey has ever been more enjoyable than travelling to a point-to-point in the Gilbert Butcher and Son blue van. Bouncing around happily in the back seat as Gilbert raced along the narrow country lanes, their banks and hedgerows choking with flowering may and cow-parsley.

Edenbridge was the best meeting as thanks to my grandmother's connection with the point-to-point committee we would be allowed to park in just about the best viewing position on the course, up against the rope running-rail between the last fence and the winning post. By climbing up onto the roof of Gilbert's van I had a boxholder's view of the gently undulating figure-of-eight track and I scrutinised every race minutely through an old pair of my grandfather's military binoculars.

Be it Edenbridge, Limpsfield, Ightham or Charing, the meetings all shared the same simple and uncomplicated atmosphere and style. All the pleasures were basic ones and the only concessions to a grandstand were farm trailers and bales of straw. There were certainly no advertising hoardings on show and definitely no corporate entertainment chalets and suites, as you will find at some point-to-point fixtures in the twenty-first century. The ice-cream vans sold Lyons Maid and dripping pineapple and strawberry Mivvies. The warm and musty-smelling beer tent could offer no iced lagers or designer labels. Only glasses, not plastic cups, of strong local bitter and cider. And the public address system, manned by farmers, was used not to warn us of an impending threat to foxhunting or the creeping urbanisation of the countryside but merely to remind some nervous double-barrelled gentleman that he was about to weigh out for the Adjacent Hunts race.

The owners, trainers and riders were generally the same local families year after year. I remember cheering on the likes of Mrs Shelagh French and Mr Paul Hacking, riding animals with names such as Cuckoo's Pet, Tearaway and Fly. I loved the thunderous sounds, the whoosh of air and the snap of gorse and twig as they galloped by. And I loved the pungent smells of horse flesh, hot leather and crushed grass.

I would be given a small float to bet with and I usually made a profit too, although not very much as the bookies invariably chalked the favourite up at odds-on and the favourite invariably won. I still loved wandering around among the bookies' pitches, listening to the patter and noise and envying them their loud clothes and their hoarse-throated, foxy-faced argot and style.

After the racing was over we would walk across the fields to my grandmother's house, where the dining-room cobwebs had been temporarily swept away and the best Crown Derby brought out from the cupboards. We would be served an elaborate tea of manicured sandwiches, cakes and scones. And I would tell Mrs Tanner about my winners and losers and together we would discuss other and bigger races to come.

In the summer of 1964 my grandmother, then aged 87, made her final visit to the Derby. And I went too, escaping from school for the day and joining the vast holiday crowd spilling out over Epsom Downs. I adored Epsom then and I still love it now. I loved Tattenham Hill and Tattenham Corner and the gypsies and the funfair and the noise and laughter and passion and the whole magical, tactile thrill of it all. When I grew up I would spend much of my time – too much time, a bank manager would say – trying to re-create that mood at Cheltenham, Sandown, Newbury and Kempton Park. As a boy, and then later on as a teenager, I found it – albeit in smaller measures than on Derby Day – at my local courses. At Lingfield, Plumpton and Wye. At Folkestone and Lewes.

Lewes racecourse, which closed down in 1966, was bare and basic and high up on the Downs, and offered only the most primitive accommodation, but I thought it was paradise. One rainy summer's day in 1963 I stood there loyally by the rails, nursing a broken arm while cheering my heart out as the then 27-year-old Lester Piggott rode a four-timer, spearheaded by a horse called Glamorgan, who I think was trained at Arundel by Gordon Smyth.

I remember the car park at Lewes and men playing the three-card trick behind some Southdown buses and two men fighting over a woman behind a horsebox and one of them pulling a knife. And I remember the shouting racecard and *Sporting Life* salesmen. And other sly-looking men in Flash Harry shades and sheepskin coats who, my grandmother grandly informed me, were spivs and touts. And who sold 'confidential form guides' in sealed brown envelopes. Further and better particulars of which could only be obtained by the production of a few, crisp, ten-shilling notes. By the end of the afternoon those self-same form guides, purchased by the gullible and the unwary, would be lying abandoned on the chalky grass, along with all the other discarded racing pages, fag packets, losing betting tickets and scraps of form.

I remember the first time I went inside the Members' Bar at Lewes. I remember the cigarette smoke and the raised glasses and the bottled beers along the counter. The whisky, brandy and gin and an intimation too of champagne for your higher-ups and better-offs. I remember tall, suave men in trilbies and small, brash men with loud ties and impressively upholstered ladies with bouffant hair and Christine Keeler heels, wearing rather more lipstick and eyeliner than was generally seen in Tunbridge Wells.

I couldn't have expressed it in so many words at the time but I think I was beginning to realise that betting and racing was sexy. And that some aspects of the Turf had something in common with Jayne Mansfield's wiggle and Leslie Phillips's laugh and the ambiguous newspaper reports, not explained to primary-school children, of the Profumo affair and The Headless Man. It's a sensuality that's never gone away, no matter how scrubbed and virtuous some modern racing advertising campaigns have become.

If you've ever experienced lust or desire at a wedding or funeral you should try visiting a race meeting. Dress up, back a winner, buy a bottle and feel the hormonal excitement pumping through you. You don't have to be at one of the bigger courses either. In the right company and with the right amount of money in your pocket you can enjoy the same thrill at Brighton, Fontwell or Folkestone.

I've always had an especial fondness for Folkestone, particularly in winter. I loved its old wooden runners and riders board, its white-painted grandstand and outdoor spirits bar and its general air of charmingly rural dilapidation. As a supposed adult I've been back many times since. Shivering outside on the muddy grass with the sun setting and the horses' breath standing out on the frosty air.

Go to Folkestone on a Monday afternoon in December and the last race, the getting-out stakes, still always seems to be a novice hurdle. With one or two punters having a go and a bookie's runner dashing down the line and the tic-tac men waving their arms around frantically. And then after it's over, win or lose, there's always just time for one last brandy or sloe gin before hurrying across the field to Westenhanger station to catch the train back up to London. Travelling to Charing Cross, naturally, on assuming one's grown-up career of dilettante, in first class.

Most of the horses that ran down at Folkestone in the 1960s were little better than point-to-pointers and to keep up with the progress of the top jumpers I continued to be dependent on the television. And occasionally the wireless too. One late April afternoon in 1965, Gilbert Butcher and I huddled around his transistor radio in the back of the firm's van. We were in the middle of an outing to the Limpsfield point-to-point but we wanted to hear Peter Bromley's BBC radio commentary on the Whitbread Gold Cup at Sandown Park. One of the runners was an eight-year-old bay steeplechaser who had already joined the ranks of the immortals. And he wasn't called Mill House.

CHAPTER EIGHT

Between 1949 and 1957 the National Hunt Festival was dominated by one man – Dr Michael Vincent O'Brien. The finest trainer, jumping or flat, of the twentieth century and the Godfather of the modern Irish racing and breeding industries.

The Honorary Doctor won the 1948, 1949 and 1950 Cheltenham Gold Cups with Cottage Rake, one of only three triple winners of the great race. He also won the 1953 running with Knock Hard. In the same era he won three successive Champion Hurdles with Hatton's Grace (1949–51), ten divisions of the Gloucestershire Hurdle for novices and three successive Grand Nationals with three different horses (1953–55).

In 1957 O'Brien turned his attention to high stakes flat racing and his fellow countryman T.W., or Tom, Dreaper succeeded him as the annual March nemesis of the English. Dreaper had already won one Gold Cup in 1946 with Mrs J.V. Rank's Prince Regent, who had been ridden by Tim Hyde, father of the legendary breeder and horse dealer Timmie Hyde of Camas Park Stud in County Tipperary.

Dreaper went on to win four more runnings of the Blue Riband – three of them with the incomparable Arkle, the greatest steeplechaser of all time – and in a career spanning 30 years he won 26 Cheltenham Festival races in total. As well as two Mackeson Gold Cups, a Massey Ferguson Gold Cup, two Hennessy Gold Cups, a Whitbread, a King George and no less than ten renewals of the Irish National.

Horsemen and horse dealers to their fingertips, Dreaper and O'Brien personified their countrymen and women's remarkable empathy with the Turf and their unrivalled capacity to nurture and train the racehorses in their care. The two men shared many outwardly similar characteristics too. They both appeared to be quiet and softly spoken characters in 1950s Philip Larkin-style hats and coats, modestly, if purposefully, going about their business in the manner of an Irish country doctor or vet. But in each case that shy and unassuming demeanour was a deceptive façade.

Dreaper may not have shared the County Cork-born O'Brien's canny command of the betting ring but he was every bit as sharp and quick-witted. It was said that he could always tell which of the group of unbroken three year olds grazing in a field was the one to buy and at what price and, just like O'Brien, he was able to plot a horse's development to perfection. Never imposing one blanket training regime on the whole string but devising and implementing an individual programme for each animal. He seemed to know precisely when his young charges were ready to step up a level and he was nearly infallible when it came to pitching them in against the best.

Tom Dreaper trained from Greenogue stables in the small village of Killsallaghan roughly 15 miles north of Dublin. His son Jim, who took over the yard when his father retired in 1974 and whom I met 16 years later, told me that T.W. 'liked to pretend that he was really just a farmer. And that the horses just happened to go with the farm like the cows and sheep or even like the family pets.'

The atmosphere at Greenogue was a peaceful and unhurried one. There was none of the loud-voiced bull and bluster you would find at some English training establishments. And you wouldn't have seen a lot of vets and white-coated lab technicians either, dashing this way and that with their equine blood samples. Jim Dreaper also confided that while his father would've been 'amused and mildly intrigued' by modern hi-tech training methods he wouldn't have given them much credence when it came to preparing his chasers. T.W., like his great English counterpart Fulke Walwyn, was the kind of man who believed that if he couldn't tell how well or how fit his horses were just by walking into their boxes and running his practised eye over their coats and his hand over their precious legs then, frankly, he might as well give up training altogether.

The horses were exercised at Greenogue by being hacked and cantered over a mile gallop around the fields. They started off learning to jump by being schooled over a row of miniature fences but they were frequently taken away to be schooled on a racecourse too. Perhaps the yard's most famous feature was the daily tea-time feed, a hearty mix which included oats, mash, fresh eggs and Guinness.

The training regime may have seemed a benign one but beneath that self-deprecating exterior Dreaper was intensely competitive. He had his own confidential network of spies and talent spotters – 'Paddy down the country' as Jim Dreaper called them – who would keep him informed of which farmer or horse breeder had a handsome young prospect in his barn or a promising point-to-pointer in his field. In the 1980s the best of these prospects would become automatic targets for English bloodstock agents, but 40 years ago they remained a private secret shared by T.W. and a few other well-informed figures in the Irish racing milieu.

Dreaper's patrons ranged, famously, from Arkle's owner, the Duchess of Westminster, and assorted members of the Anglo-Irish squirearchy to ordinary farmers, self-made businessmen and the gambling-mad millionairess Mrs J.V. 'Pat' Rank. What united them was not simply their money or their love of racing. They all understood that it took time and patience to develop a top-class racehorse and to ensure that such a horse would enjoy a long and rewarding career in training.

Dreaper and his compatriots Dan Moore and Paddy Sleator

and the Englishmen Fulke Walwyn and Fred Rimell exemplified an approach that would be followed by Fred Winter when he started training and was later adopted by Jenny Pitman. They weren't interested in playing the numbers game or buying cheap but ready-made hurdling prospects off the flat just to give some commercially minded owners a quick return on their money. Dreaper was, in his son's words, 'after looking at some great big, immature stamp of a horse in a field and seeing him as a potential two-mile champion chaser or a Gold Cup or Irish National winner in four or five years time.'

By looking after their jumpers and hurdlers and bringing them back at the highest level season after season, the Dreaper stable were able to establish a rapport with the racing community on both sides of the Irish Sea, who love nothing better than to identify with a great and courageous horse and watch it return to do battle time and time again. Arkle may have sported the colours of a duchess but to his adoring public he was running for every half-skint punter and racing lover from Cork to Coleraine and from Salisbury to Stockton-on-Tees.

We first saw Arkle in Britain at the 1962 Cheltenham November meeting where the then five-year-old gelding won a two-and-a-half-mile novice steeplechase. Arkle returned to the Cotswolds the following March, running in and winning the Broadway Chase, that classic three-mile test for novices that in those days was run as the fourth event on the first day of the meeting. It was always an informative form guide to the future, as I had come to understand by scrutinising past results and seeing how the principals had progressed over the following seasons.

The SunAlliance Chase, as it's been known since 1973, has been won by a number of future Gold Cup winners but there've been just as many embryonic champions who've gone down to unexpected and ignominious defeat. Silver Buck. Little Owl. Burrough Hill Lad. Forgive 'N' Forget. Mr Mulligan. It's quite a list. And one that has encouraged some trainers to bypass the contest in recent years and even to run their best novices against the older horses in the big one. Jim Dreaper ran Carvill's Hill in the 1989 Gold Cup even though the massive bay had only run four times over fences. His father employed similar tactics with French Tan and Leap Frog but when it came to Arkle the master trainer preferred to approach the summit by the time-honoured route.

The 1963 Festival may've been dominated by Mill House and the emphatic manner of his victory in the Gold Cup, but no bookie or punter could ignore the significance of Arkle's fluent six-length win on the opening afternoon. Here was another young horse with untold potential and one whose trainer, undaunted by what Mill House might achieve, had immediately nominated him as a Gold Cup candidate for 1964.

The two chasers met for the first time in the Hennessy Gold Cup at Newbury at the end of November. It was a frosty winter's afternoon, ideal for watching *Grandstand* on TV: three races from Newbury followed by motor-cycle scramble ('And where is Jeff Smith?' Murray Walker would yell) and then Kent Walton and the wrestling on the other side. The big race was the best, of course, and it was Mill House, conceding five pounds, who scored a somewhat illusory victory, coming home eight lengths clear of Happy Spring with Arkle, who had stumbled on landing at the third-last fence, another three-quarters of a length away.

Mill House went on to record an effortless triumph in the King George VI Chase at Kempton on Boxing Day, his victory tasting as good to me as the wine I was allowed to drink at lunch, and his continuing domination of the steeplechasing firmament seemed assured. My patriotic worship of the Big Horse and his imposing, almost medieval power continued unabated but I suspect that like countless others of his admirers, I was overlooking the uncompetitive nature of his latest success. The King George had been a three-horse race and his nearest pursuer had been Blue Dolphin, a specialist two-miler. The margin of superiority was deceptive and for Mill House the era of swaggering monopoly was drawing to a close.

Tom Dreaper had taken Arkle back to Greenogue after the Hennessy and schooled him, smoothing his rough edges. The horse scored comfortable victories in Ireland's two big staying steeplechases, the Thyestes at Gowran Park in January and the Leopardstown Chase a month later. Arkle was now as ready as he ever would be and his canny handler and his great horseman of a jockey Pat Taaffe were convinced that he would have too much class and speed for his English rival.

It would be difficult to exaggerate the spine-tingling sense of anticipation that preceded that 1964 Festival. I could feel it all and I was only nine years old and reading the racing pages and watching what I could on television.

Tom Dreaper began the meeting in ominously triumphant fashion when he saddled Flyingbolt to win the opening division of the Gloucestershire Hurdle by ten lengths. This magnificent-looking chestnut five year old had the kind of raking stride and high cruising speed that suggested that over maybe two or two and a half miles he might even be a match for his illustrious stable companion. They never met in a level weights championship but over the next few golden years, Flyingbolt's name would add very near comparable lustre to Dreaper's and Ireland's reputation.

My usual scrambling run home from school got me back just in time to see Dreaper and Pat Taaffe score again with Ben Stack in the two-mile Champion Chase. Ben Stack, like Arkle, was owned by the Duchess of Westminster and the race was a bad omen for Fulke Walwyn and Willie Robinson, trainer and jockey of Mill House, as they could manage only third place with their own much fancied runner Irish Imp.

Walwyn's spirits were lifted slightly on the second afternoon when he saddled the 50–1 outsider Kirriemuir to finish third in the Champion Hurdle. Kirriemuir, who was only four years old at the time, stayed on strongly up the hill and was only a few lengths behind the Scottish-trained winner Magic Court.

Kirriemuir won the race 12 months later while Another Flash, a previous Champion Hurdler himself (who'd also finished third twice) finished second in 1964. More pointers to remember for my racing and gambling future. Horses who run well at

Cheltenham once will invariably run well there again and again, while the reverse is equally true. A few top-class animals like Silver Buck, Desert Orchid and One Man have managed to overcome their aversion to Cheltenham at the fourth or fifth attempt but they are very much the exception to the rule.

Back in 1964 the normal Tuesday to Thursday programme had been re-scheduled to take place, most unusually, from Thursday to Saturday and so of course for the first time since 1961 I was able to watch the whole two-hour Gold Cup transmission live on television. The black and white pictures captured perfectly the bright sunlight and bitter cold of that March day. There were still piles of unmelted snow around the in-field and on the top of Cleeve Hill and there was even a dramatic flurry of snow minutes before the Gold Cup began.

If the 1964 Blue Riband was to be a landmark in the history of National Hunt racing, it was also to be a momentous occasion in the history of BBC sport. Peter O'Sullevan, of course, was in pole position with his good friend and colleague Clive Graham describing the horses in the parade ring. Just four runners went to post for the big race with only the 1960 winner Pas Seul and Stan Mellor's mount King's Nephew daring to take on the favourites, but there was no need for the commentators to simulate bogus excitement. Their gradual paddock build-up carried a steadily accumulating weight and tension as camera movement and voice-over contributed to a mood of awed reverence for the principal competitors and thrilling anticipation of the contest to come. All the trials were over now and the talk and the preparation was nearly at an end. The race was here and I just wanted to live in every second of the present and cherish it to the hilt.

As Arkle and Mill House walked around at opposite ends of the paddock I remember looking at the Big Horse, massive and contemptuous, and wondering whether he realised the significance of what was about to take place. Might he look his opponent, smaller but oozing class, in the eye? And if he did would he recognise that this was the rival he had to break and that the coming struggle between them would be the defining moment of their racing lives?

There are special videos available these days enabling you to relive every fence and every detail of Arkle's Cheltenham victories but it's a tribute once again to the power of television and to the impression those races made on me when I say that I could remember almost every nuance of that 1964 Gold Cup, and recite much of O'Sullevan's climactic commentary, word for word, long before I saw the race again on film.

The punters sent Mill House off as the 13–8 favourite with Arkle at 7–4. The other two contestants were virtually ignored. Mill House made the running in the early stages, but for the first circuit the race was close and even, with little more than six lengths covering the field. The real race began on the second circuit.

As soon as they started out down the hill into the country for the second time, Willie Robinson tried to seize the initiative by pushing Mill House into a clear and emphatic lead. It was a tactic I was to remember and see again in another of Fulke Walwyn's great chasers, Ten Plus, when he took on Desert Orchid in 1989. Robinson was trying to consistently and extravagantly outjump his opponent on the far side and get Arkle off the bit even before they started the crucial downhill run towards home. And Mill House's jumping *was* brilliant, but while Pas Seul and King's Nephew were soon in trouble, Arkle – so quick and so agile – could not be shaken off.

As they approached the top of the hill for the last time the tension was almost unbearable. I'd begun the race perched on the edge of my chair and then moved down to the carpet to be nearer to the screen. By the end I would be on my hands and knees and praying for a different outcome.

Peter O'Sullevan was faultless throughout. As well as his natural grasp of rhythm he also possessed an actor's intuitive sense of timing. He knew that he couldn't afford to peak too soon and that he had to allow the contest room to build. So on the first circuit you could almost feel him keeping the horses on a loose rein but then just after halfway his voice started to rise and a new mood of urgency took over.

With less than a mile left to run he began to reel the race in and to reel us in with it. 'And it's the Big Two now,' he called, as they raced over the brow of the hill, Mill House between two and three lengths clear. 'As they run down the hill to the third-last fence . . . the Big Horse . . . ' – he'd said it – ' . . . Mill House with Arkle closing on him. And it's Mill House and Willie Robinson, Arkle and Pat Taaffe . . . '

And then O'Sullevan said something else that sent a shiver up my spine then and still does now almost 40 years later. He described something he had heard and that I have heard countless times since standing down on the lawn at Cheltenham. 'And Pat Taaffe being shouted for from the stands now,' he said. 'Irish voices really beginning to call for him now as he starts to make up ground . . . ' Any regular Festival-goer must have heard those same Irish voices. The true believers calling home other gambled-on Irish favourites, from Parkhill and Mr Kildare to Golden Cygnet and Bobsline, from Mister Donovan to Danoli and Imperial Call, and from Florida Pearl to Istabraq. Beckoning the banker to return to the winners' enclosure in safety and in triumph.

At the third-last fence in 1964 Mill House was fractionally the better jumper, Arkle seeming to peck slightly on landing and Mill House away powerfully and well and maybe once again three to four lengths clear and still travelling.

Arkle was on the far side now, Mill House on the inner, and this was the moment when Pat Taaffe clearly realised he had to ask his horse, had to sit down and ride him and find out just how good he really was. And what an answer he got as, like Bobsline tracking Noddy's Ryde in the appropriately named Arkle Trophy in 1984, Arkle quickened like a champion. His acceleration was so marked and so immediate that the three- or four-length gap between himself and Mill House was swiftly closed.

By the penultimate fence the two horses were nearly level. Stride for stride. Neck and neck. O'Sullevan saw it all. 'They've got two fences left to jump now. And they're both still full of running. Still going great guns, both of them. And this is it . . . '

And it was it too, but whereas 12 months before Willie Robinson and Mill House had strode over that second-last fence invincible and alone, this time they had Pat Taaffe and Arkle upsides them, Taaffe still just shaking up the reins as Robinson reached for his whip. Mill House touched down fractionally ahead but as they made that dramatic turn into the home straight there was nothing in it.

'And this is the race now,' continued O'Sullevan. 'It's Arkle on the stands side for Ireland. And Mill House for England on the far side. And this is it. With Arkle just taking the lead as they come to the last fence . . .' O'Sullevan's voice was rising emotionally; he could see what was coming. 'It's going to be Arkle if he jumps it . . . ' And he did jump it. Magnificently. Mill House fought back with everything as he tried to challenge again on the run-in, but halfway up that daunting uphill finish it was clear that Arkle had his measure and that the Big Horse wouldn't get by. In the final 50 yards Arkle seemed to accelerate again, drawing away into history and into a class of his own. '*This* is the champion,' called O'Sullevan evocatively. 'This is the best we've seen for a *long* time.'

He was absolutely right of course but at first I could hardly believe it and I don't think many other British racing enthusiasts (or, as I later discovered, racing professionals) could quite believe what Arkle had done to the super-fit and strong Mill House that March day in 1964. I was almost in tears for my defeated hero. I watched the pictures and listened to O'Sullevan describe the tumultuous reception that Arkle was receiving. 'There was no conceivable excuse,' the commentator reminded us, but naive as not quite ten year olds invariably are, I clung to the idea that next time . . . one day . . . if not at Cheltenham then somewhere else . . . the result might be different.

CHAPTER NINE

After the 1964 Cheltenham Festival, Arkle went on to win the Irish National at Fairyhouse under 12 stone. The BBC showed the RTE commentary with the superlative Michael O'Hehir, the Michael MacLiamorr of televised sport, exhorting them home. That same April, Mill House finished second in the Whitbread Gold Cup carrying 12 st. 7 lb. Both horses could now regularly expect to be set crushing tasks by the handicapper and it was Arkle's turn to heft 12 st. 7 lb the 1964 Hennessy, though that didn't stop him winning by 10 lengths, another staggering success.

The Irish champion went on to contest Cheltenham's new Massey Ferguson Gold Cup in December – another TV highlight of my winter Saturdays – where he performed heroically in running third, beaten a short head and a length, to Dan Moore's high-class mare Flying Wild. The race was nearly half a mile short of Arkle's preferred distance of 3 miles plus and the Duchess's star was required to carry 12 st. 10 lb and concede a back-breaking 32 lb to the winner.

Due to bad weather warnings, Arkle and Mill House both bypassed the 1964 King George VI Chase at Kempton, which was won by the nine-year-old Frenchman's Cove, who'd been third in Mill House's first Gold Cup. At least there was a full programme of televised sport. Cold turkey and bubble and squeak weren't the same without the Boxing Day racing.

As March drew round once again there was much talk from chivalrous, romantic and patriotic writers – like Johnny Lawrence in my parents' *Telegraph* – of how in a differently run race and with experience and forewarning of his opponent's strengths and weaknesses (what weaknesses?), Mill House might be able to turn the tables on Arkle but I wasn't buying it. However much I idolised Mill House I think I was already beginning to identify as much if not more with his charismatic opponent. And perhaps I sensed too that chivalrous and romantic racing writers are usually as hopelessly doomed and inaccurate in their predictions as propagandists for other chivalrous but doomed causes.

The 1965 Festival returned to its normal Tuesday to Thursday slot in the calendar and Tom Dreaper again won the opening Gloucestershire Hurdle, this time with another promising young chasing type called Dicky May. The stable followed up 24 hours later when Flyingbolt slaughtered the opposition in the two-mile Cotswold Novices Chase (nowadays the Arkle Trophy). But English hearts had been lifted by the devastating performance of Colonel Billy Whitbread's Dunkirk in the two-mile champion chase and Fulke Walwyn and Willie Robinson scored another famous Cheltenham victory in the Champion Hurdle when Kirriemuir – older, stronger and more experienced than the previous year – outclassed a horse called Spartan General, who was ridden by Terry Biddlecombe. The Queen Mother's runner, Worcran, was placed third.

Another frantic and breathless lunge up the hill from school got me back just in time to see the 1965 Gold Cup from start to finish, its outcome and import seeming vastly more important to me than the results of the Eleven Plus exam I'd just taken. The weather and conditions that March day were almost identical to those of 12 months before. The same bitter cold and hard, bright sunlight. The same baggy grey coats in the crowd by the rails. Even the same ambulancemen. Once again there were just the four runners, with the Australian cross-country chaser Stony Crossing and the ten-year-old Caduval the only other horses prepared to take on the champions.

Mill House looked every bit as strong and handsome as he had done in 1963 and '64 and for the first two-thirds of the race his jumping was as good as it gets. But then so was Arkle's and when they started up the hill on the far side for the final time, it was Arkle who was fractionally ahead. Then Mill House ranged up alongside him at the fourth from home and for a few, illusory, moments his supporters in the stands were able to convince themselves that he was going the better. They swung left-handed and began the downhill race towards home.

It's only when you walk the course at Cheltenham that you can really appreciate just how intimidating the downhill fences must be at racing speed but Arkle took them quite literally in his stride and surely no Gold Cup winner can ever have travelled faster or more fluently over the downhill section than he did in 1965. He sped over both the third- and second-last fences and as they galloped towards the turn it was obvious to everyone that the race was effectively over.

Arkle's pace was relentless, his enjoyment plain to see, but behind him Mill House was labouring and unable to even get the favourite off the bit. Arkle, in Peter O'Sullevan's words, had simply opened up and changed gear like a sports car. He produced a mighty leap at the last and then stormed up the hill like the absolute superstar that he was. In 1964 the winning distance had been five lengths. This time it was more like 20 and whereas the Big Horse had gone down to honourable defeat in their first Gold Cup bout, the rematch saw him broken and broken utterly.

Arkle went on next to win the 1965 Whitbread Gold Cup at Sandown in April, carrying the same welter burden of 12 st. 7 lb that had proved just too much for Mill House the year before. Then the following November he won a second successive Hennessy Gold Cup by 15 lengths under a similar weight. These were unprecedented achievements – no horse in the modern era has yet come close to matching them – and earlier that month he'd flayed Mill House again in the new Gallaher Gold Cup also run at Sandown. Defeat for the Big Horse was followed by the news that Fulke Walwyn's eight year old had injured himself and would be out for the rest of the season. His departure from the scene felt like a symbolic summation of just how comprehensively he'd been vanquished on the track.

Arkle's domination of the steeplechasing world was now as total as that of any sporting phenomenon in any sphere from Nicklaus on the golf course to Pelé on the soccer pitch and Ali in the ring. And no book or fable and certainly no lesson from school could begin to match his hold on my imagination. Others might have had a specific team to follow or a player to worship but to me this horse was everything.

Colonel Billy Whitbread, every inch a sportsman and traditionalist in the John Lawrence mould, decided that somebody had to take Arkle on. He was determined that the British public should have a spectacle to warm to in the King George VI Chase at Kempton over Christmas. So the Colonel committed his brilliant two-mile champion Dunkirk to the race, erroneously believing, as many others have done since, that a specialist two-miler might have a chance against the Gold Cup horses around Kempton's tight three-mile track. Whitbread's and his trainer Peter Cazalet's boldness ended in tragedy. Dunkirk, who was trying to match strides with Arkle at the time, fell at the fifth-last fence and broke his neck. Arkle went on to win the race by ten lengths.

The 1965–66 jumping season seemed to belong exclusively to Tom Dreaper and Pat Taaffe. As well as Arkle's three English victories before the turn of the year, they saddled Flyingbolt to win the new two-mile Black and White Whisky Gold Cup at Ascot in November and then they brought him back over in December to scoop the third running of the Massey Ferguson over the new course at Cheltenham. Flyingbolt carried 12 st. 6 lb that day and his 15-length winning margin over a field of smart two-and-a-half-mile chasers led by Solbina and Scottish Memories didn't begin to reflect his superiority.

I was beginning to recognise similarities in all of Tom Dreaper's great chasers: Arkle, Flyingbolt, Ben Stack, Dicky May. They all had that same galloping power and strength. The rhythmic jumping and the ground gained in the air. There were similarities amongst the riders too. Liam McLoughlin. Sean Barker. Tos Taaffe. Pat himself. They all wore the same old-fashioned thick jerseys and fawn-coloured waterproof britches and they had the same kind of helmets with the big chin straps. There were no skin-tight, aero-dynamic silks. Not on an Irish jump jockey in 1965.

Arkle and Flyingbolt completed their Festival preparations in different races at Leopardstown in February and on the first day of the 1966 March meeting it was Flyingbolt who captured the headlines and the admiration of the crowd as he carried off the Champion Chase by 15 lengths.

Twenty-four hours later this outstanding horse was saddled again in the Champion Hurdle. And he was still in front and still going strongly as they jumped the second-last flight at the bottom of the hill but in this high-speed hurdle race company Pat Taaffe's upright Master of Foxhounds' style of riding was shown up cruelly. The polished hurdle-race specialist Johnny Haine was riding the quick and classy Salmon Spray for Bob Turnell and the combination sat waiting in behind Flyingbolt on the turn into the straight and then pounced at the last. Haine's low carriage and rhythmical style impelled Salmon Spray up the hill while Flyingbolt's rider looked like an ungainly amateur trying to keep his balance. Taaffe, though, would have the last laugh on his detractors.

The next day's Gold Cup – 12 March 1966 – was expected to be little more than an exhibition round for Arkle. With no Mill House to do battle with this time, 'Himself' was faced with just four inferior opponents, all of whom would've needed to receive at least two stone to make a proper race of it.

The champion was sent off at 1–10 by the bookies, meaning that you would have had to bet ten pounds to win one, but for one brief moment his worshippers' hearts came to a stop when he seemed to forget to take off at the fence in front of the stands on the first circuit. He ploughed through the jump so absolutely that his survival was scarcely credible to behold, but somehow the hero stayed on his feet and his canny rider, now displaying all the advantages of his experience in the hunting field, remained glued to the saddle. Next time around Arkle was more than 20 lengths clear and he skipped over the fence as if the error had never happened and romped up the hill to what was to be his final Cheltenham victory.

The fans cheered and cheered him to the rooftops. He was truly l'Empereur. And he had just made steeplechasing history once again by becoming the only horse since Cottage Rake in the 1950s and, until Best Mate in 2004, only the third horse ever to win three successive runnings of the Cheltenham Gold Cup. Only the mighty Golden Miller, the colossus of the 1930s, was fit to mention in the same breath.

Arkle didn't race again that season, although Flyingbolt won the Irish National under 12 st. 7 lb. By the time jump racing resumed again in the autumn it was not Arkle's rivals on the track but the handicapper who eventually engineered his defeat. The triple-Gold Cup winner was asked to carry an ever more punitive series of weights against the featherweight burdens of a new generation of up and coming jumping stars.

In the 1966 Hennessy, Arkle went down by a head to the seven-year-old grey Stalbridge Colonist to whom he was conceding a massive 2 st. 5lb. What A Myth, a future Gold Cup winner, got the same weight allowance and finished a length away in third. Then in the 1966 King George, the great horse was beaten by a length by Dormant whom he'd annihilated in the Gold Cup in March. Dormant, was receiving a stone and a half that day but the weight difference alone didn't explain Arkle's defeat. When Pat Taaffe dismounted he could tell at once that his horse was lame and had probably been hurting all the way through the race. Taaffe feared that Arkle had broken down badly and there was no question of him going straight back to Ireland that night. He would have to stay in the racecourse stables at Kempton Park. X-rays were taken of his off-fore leg and they revealed an injury to his pedal bone – the pedal bone being the bone in a horse's foot which they press down on when they jump.

We didn't know it then but Arkle's career was over. His personal vet flew across from Ireland the following day. There were lengthy examinations and a plaster cast was made to protect the vulnerable leg from the knee down to the hoof. Arkle, the most intelligent and biddable of steeplechasers, submitted to the treatment with equanimity. He remained at Kempton for nine weeks while the vets waited for the cracked bone to heal and while he was there he received hundreds of letters, presents and get-well cards along with regular visits from the Duchess of Westminster, who travelled down to see him from her Eaton Hall home in Cheshire or her houses in Ireland and Scotland.

Finally, on 26 February 1967, Arkle returned to Kilsallaghan. Dreaper and his team spent the next 18 months trying to nurse the triple champion back to peak fitness but he never raced again. In October 1968 the Duchess retired him to a paddock on her stud at Bryanstown in County Kildare, where a grey mare called Meg was his constant companion. He made a few celebrity appearances, responding to the crowds with majesty and élan, but as he got older he suffered increasingly from arthritis. And on 31 May 1970 he was put down.

Many years later I walked into Leopardstown racecourse on the edges of Dublin and climbed the stairs to the Hall of Fame on the first floor. I stood in front of the biggest display case and looked again at Arkle's colours and at his trophies and cups. And I looked at the letters to Dreaper and Pat Taaffe and at Arkle's equine passport and at the telegrams from the Duchess and the President of Ireland. And I saw the old black and white newspaper pictures of Arkle doing battle with Mill House and others at Cheltenham, Newbury, Leopardstown and Fairyhouse. And reliving those memories and remembering those days brought a lump to my throat and I am not one whit embarrassed to admit it.

Even aged nine I think I had realised that Arkle was the best horse I'd ever seen and probably the best I'd ever be likely to see, but that didn't stop me from yearning and searching for another racing experience with the power and intensity to rekindle the memory of that fabulous era. I found it eventually, although it would take me almost 20 years. And when it came it was surrounded with more drama and emotion than I could possibly have imagined.

Mill House returned to the racetrack in 1967 and with two smooth wins under his belt in preparatory races he was sent into the '67 Gold Cup as the 5–2 favourite. Willie Robinson was injured that year and his place was taken by a grim-looking David Nicholson. The Big Horse was almost his old self as he led the field, jumping superbly on the first circuit, but at the final open ditch at the top of the hill second time around, his legs gave way on landing and Nicholson was unseated. The horse he'd been leading at the time was Terry Biddlecombe's mount Woodland Venture, who was the subsequent winner of the race.

Mill House did succeed in winning the 1967 Whitbread at Sandown carrying top weight of 11 st. 11 lb against a 15-strong field. That day the much-loved old champion was cheered to the rafters, but if there were some who still dreamed that the Big Horse might yet make a triumphant return to Cheltenham, their hopes were finally buried in March 1968.

Once again Mill House, now 11 years old, started as the Gold Cup favourite and once again he looked outstandingly strong and well and jumped like a champion through the first half of the race. There was to be no happy ending though. At the 15th fence, the penultimate open ditch this time, he over-jumped and came down. Willie Robinson, reunited with his old friend, was given no chance of staying in the saddle. Perhaps the horse was too old. Perhaps you can never come back from injury at the highest level. Or perhaps the memory of those two crushing defeats by Arkle had burned their way too deeply into the animal's Cheltenham consciousness. As in 1967 the horse he was leading when he fell went on to win the race. And with a final painful irony that horse, Fort Leney, was trained by Tom Dreaper and ridden by Pat Taaffe.

Jim Dreaper won the Cheltenham Gold Cup in 1975 with Ten Up, who was owned by the Duchess, and he won two other races at the same Festival meeting but his father Tom had only recently retired and inevitably the '75 triumphs were seen as much as his final swan song as a vindication of the abilities of his son.

Jim has trained many big-race winners in Ireland, including three memorable victories in the Irish National with Brown Lad, one of the best horses never to win a Gold Cup, but he has not had another winner at Cheltenham since that hat-trick more than 25 years ago. In 1995 he sent over Merry Gale, who jumped superbly and led the field for two-thirds of the Gold Cup before tiring and finishing third. And at that same Festival meeting Dreaper saddled a giant tank of a horse called Harcon in the SunAlliance Chase, the race that had been won in their time by both Arkle and Ten Up.

Grown men – legendary Irish racing lovers and one legendary Scottish sportswriter amongst them – fingered their betting slips nervously and talked in hushed and awed tones of Harcon's promise and reputation. Was he not Arkle incarnate, returned at last to Prestbury Park? Alas not. Harcon was about twice the size of Arkle for a start off and only about a third as quick. He performed creditably, finishing an honourable second on ground a shade too firm for him thanks to a biting, drying wind. Then the following season he got an injury. And was barely seen again.

You sometimes feel that Jim Dreaper almost expects to be disappointed when he gets a good horse and that, even if only subconsciously, he half welcomes the disappointment in advance, sparing him the torment of trying to live up to the unsurpassed Cheltenham record of his father.

Greenogue remains a friendly, welcoming stable and a thriving farm. And a place of pilgrimage too. But the most compelling pictures on the hall walls are still the old black and white photographs from the 1960s and early '70s. The past, it seems, continues to hold the present in thrall.

The end of the Arkle–Mill House era coincided with the final years of my childhood. So it was perhaps appropriate that roughly seven months after Arkle's last run my grandmother, my first and foremost racing tutor, died.

Alert and vigorous right up to her 90th summer, Mrs Tanner had remained in regular contact with her bookmakers. If I remember rightly her last big winner was Spaniard's Mount, ridden by Doug Smith, who won the 1967 Wokingham Stakes at Royal Ascot at odds of 100–6. Then the following month Grandma had a fall, that accident most dreaded by elderly ladies and gentlemen. She broke her hip and as a consequence of her inevitable incapacity was removed from The Thorns and taken to the Kent and Sussex Hospital at Pembury near Tunbridge Wells, where she subsequently suffered a stroke and where a week later complications set in until she finally died in her sleep on 12 August 1967.

The last time I saw her was on a sultry August afternoon and she was sitting up in bed, in her over-heated and medicinal-smelling ward, unable to speak. Yet from the fierce clarity with which she looked me in the eye I was left in no doubt that she understood everything I was saying.

Her once-beautiful auburn hair was now long and white and tangled much like Miss Havisham's. For a while, as I talked about horses and races, I held her hand and my mother brushed her hair for her gently with one of the fine ivory-backed hairbrushes that she'd insisted on having brought from home. When the time came to leave I looked back at her over my shoulder, trying to smile as best I could. She was still looking me in the eye with the same level intensity. And I felt as if she was trying to nod at me and to send me on my way with her blessing. Out into the world and on with my life.

The moment reminded me of my earliest visits to see Mrs Tanner in Edenbridge with my mother. When we left in the afternoons the old lady would always come out to the gate with us to say goodbye. And whatever the weather and whatever the season she would stand in the lane and continue to watch and wave as we walked away. Standing there with her hand raised until we had finally turned the corner at the top of the hill and were out of sight.

How much I wish that I had known Grandma when she was younger or I was older. And how much I would love to have responded to her stories about Crepello and Cottage Rake, Golden Miller and Hyperion by telling her of the champions that I have been moved by.

I cherish her memory.

CHAPTER TEN

The escapist character of a racing lover is not simply created by positive encouragement. It can also be borne out of a reaction to disapproval and a rejection of attempts to impose conformity and stamp out dissent. And nothing did more to encourage my trajectory as a dissenter than the crushingly conformist and authoritarian regime of the Judd Grammar School for boys in Tonbridge, Kent.

In March 1965 I passed the Eleven Plus. Six months later I set out nervously for the bus stop by Leigh village green. A kind of social and academic apartheid was about to begin and it was the excessive detail of my new school uniform that was the visible symbol of my supposedly privileged status. Former primary-school friends and enemies now embarking on a secondary-modern career had to wear a black or grey jacket and black trousers. They wore a tie but were bareheaded and carried their books in a kitbag. I had to carry a tax inspector's briefcase and wear grey flannel trousers with turn-ups and a navy blue blazer with the school badge on the top pocket. I had to wear grey V-necked pullovers with a maroon border and the maroon and · navy-blue school tie. And, most conspicuous of all, the maroon and navy-blue school cap with badge.

There was no more reliable incitement to mockery and

violence than this detested hat. Anyone of a mind that all grammar-school boys were snobs and wankers could hardly resist such a tempting target. It was so easy to grab from behind and chuck over a wall or into a puddle or throw out of a bus window in front of the wheels of a passing car.

Things got even worse in the fourth form when we were compelled to wear a straw boater in the summer term. All very Jeeves and Wooster and Henley Regatta and good sport for the lads from the neighbouring schools, but misery for Juddians. I tried to hide my hat whenever I could but if you were caught without it by the school prefects you were immediately punished and informed that when travelling on a bus or train you still represented the school. As if the very act of using public transport could only be embarked on providing you were wearing full Juddian colours. Even if an order had gone out replacing caps and boaters with Mexican sombreros or a Tommy Cooper-style fez.

The headmaster regularly assured parents that a strict dress code was the first line of defence when it came to maintaining standards. The boys believed that it was also a nice little earner for the Governors, several of whom were suspected of being leading investors in the firm of men's outfitters that stocked our innumerable changes of gear. But then the Judd School was proud of its mercantile traditions and its founder, Sir Andrew Judd, would no doubt have applauded the shrewd exploitation of a commercial opening.

Sir Andrew had started the Skinners Company, a group of Elizabethan merchant adventurers who had opened up lucrative trade routes to Russia and the Baltic States. And Skinners Hall, Sir Andrew's legacy on Dowgate Hill in the City of London, was a sleek and polished shrine to the wealth and power of traditional pre-Thatcherite capitalism.

Once a year a select party of Juddians would be shown around these august premises, our guide encouraging us to adopt a tone of suitably reverential gratitude towards our benefactors as if they were the Charitable Grinders in *Dombey and Son*. The tour would climax with a lashing of tuck-style tea followed by the head boy calling for three cheers for our generous hosts.

The famed largesse of the Skinners was – so we were constantly assured – what made it possible for us sons of tradesmen and the shop-assistant classes to get the kind of education that the parents of public schoolboys paid dearly for. And secondary-modern 'louts and hooligans' could only dream of.

The Skinners – most of whom wouldn't have dreamed of sending their own children to a grammar school – clearly believed that, to make us work harder and achieve more, we shouldn't be pampered when it came to classrooms and facilities. The Judd School buildings were a dreary collection of late Victorian red-brick with assorted pre- and post-war prefabricated and utilitarian extensions. The chemistry and physics laboratories in particular would've looked prehistoric in Billy Bunter's time.

The school was obsessed with sport in general and rugby in particular and it was made clear from the outset that playing team games and striving for O and A level examination success was the overriding purpose of a Juddian education. We were continually reminded that passing the Eleven Plus had provided us with a precious opportunity. A lifeline to the first world. Now the pressure was really on. We had to shape up and succeed. The consequences of failure were high. Shame for the school and pariah status for the pupil, whose inadequacy would hold them back for ever more.

Expulsion was the worst. Boys who were expelled from Judd were, so we were told, cast into the outer darkness with no references. Destined in all probability to end up as travelling salesmen, living in rented accommodation in High Brooms or Rusthall, the Tunbridge Wells equivalent of the Gold Coast. The school, forever boasting of its reputation for turning out conventional and well-disciplined boys, simply wouldn't tolerate rebellion and as I came painfully to realise, it was not naturally sympathetic to skiving, gambling and the delights of the Turf.

That first September day in 1965 it was raining hard. We new boys, 64 of us in our new and unfamiliar uniforms, had been ordered to assemble in the woodwork shed. The woodwork teacher, Rodney Vincent Fricker, was a large, pompous man with a conspicuous boil on his forehead. On Friday afternoons he dressed up in full army officer gear and reappeared as Reichsführer Fricker of the Combined Cadet Corps. That September morning he was wearing a brown overall and strutting up and down between the work benches humming 'Bow Down Ye Lower Middle Classes'.

Our form masters duly arrived and read out our names and then we were marched off still in silence. My classroom was at the end of a dingy corridor. Forty brown wooden desks in five rows of eight, brown linoleum on the floors. And bare, cream-painted walls. No posters, paintings, drawings or photographs. Absolutely nothing. Just a teacher's desk and blackboard at the front and a clock at the back, which we would be ill-advised to turn around and look at.

My first-year form master was a man called Sackett, who was also the chief PE and games teacher. There was a sinister and slightly homoerotic side to Sackett. He was the hard screw. The one man that nearly every boy in the school, be they 11 or 18, was afraid of and I suspect that some of the other teachers were afraid of him too. He emanated a kind of bullying, male sexuality and he had a habit of appearing suddenly in classrooms. You'd look up and he'd be there, quietly menacing, and you'd immediately feel nervous or guilty and wonder what it was he was about to say or do next. He loved the effect he created, I'm sure. He could intimidate you by his look, manner and sarcastic tongue and, as we discovered later, by occasional terrifying bursts of temper accompanied by strictly off-the-record violence.

Sackett taught us first-year maths. It was his only non-games teaching assignment and we were the only class in the entire school to benefit from his tuition. Quite what had persuaded the headmaster that he was the ideal man for the task was unclear but it was all purgatory for me. Maths had always been my weakest subject at primary school and now the complexities of algebra and geometry were being explained by a man twice as cutting as Miss Welch and with a much stronger forearm. Sackett was deadly through the air with a board rubber at 20 paces as many in his class could testify and our Tuesday and Thursday morning double periods in his company soon became the most dreaded hours of the week.

If Sackett didn't get you in the maths lessons he had plenty of other opportunities to humiliate you in the gym. No matter what we'd been doing beforehand or what the previous lesson had been, we were permitted no more than two or three minutes to get changed for PE. And once inside the gymnasium there was an unwritten law that you had to immediately start running on the spot, frantically climbing up the wall bars or just doing something, anything, active and energetic. If Sackett came in and you were standing still – idling, loafing, dreaming of escape or whatever – you'd be in for it. Extra press-ups, long runs around the playing fields, verbal torture in front of the class. All this and more would be your reward.

In between sessions in the gym, Sackett liked to swagger up and down the school corridors in his PE kit. Short-sleeved, white Aertex shirt and black tracksuit trousers. He would often pose around like this in the classroom, doing rather intimidating muscle-stretching exercises with first one leg up on his desk then the other. At the age of 12 he terrified me. By 13 I despised him but he remained the most disturbing presence of my school life.

As well as disciplining preferably half-dressed boys, Sackett's other great passion was rugby. Our games lessons involved endless cold and muddy afternoons trundling around the school pitches. The headmaster doted on the performances of the various teams against Chislehurst and Sidcup, Dartford Grammar School, Rochester Mathematical School and other similarly worthy institutions and the results would be read out reverentially in assembly each Monday.

For the first few years we were expected to throw ourselves into all games lessons with hysterical enthusiasm but then at the age of 14 I began to develop an interest in acting and joined a local youth theatre. And as far as Sackett was concerned that identified me as some sort of hippy and poof. 'There goes one of our bigger girls,' he would say out loud to a fellow member of staff as I walked by with my non-regulation-length hair stuffed behind my ears.

As I got older Sackett's interest in me waned. I was a sixth-form arts student and clearly a write-off from the games master's point of view. He had a new generation of potential locks, props and wing three-quarters to mould and manipulate but he could still make you squirm on occasion.

One morning in 1971 four or five of us who were studying A level English were sitting in a classroom waiting for a minibus to arrive to drive us across town to the girls' grammar school. They had organised a showing of Lawrence Olivier's *Hamlet*. The play was one of our set texts and it had been arranged that we should take the morning off to see the film. It was not quite our idea of riveting, contemporary cinema but it was still an opportunity to mix with girls and a chance to miss two or three lessons. Amongst them PE.

We were sitting there waiting for our lift and chatting away harmlessly when the temperature in the room seemed to drop. We looked round nervously. And there was Sackett. Standing in the doorway.

'What are you doing?' he asked, quiet and menacing.

We started to explain about the film and English and the girls' grammar and how we'd been given permission . . .

'No you haven't,' said Sackett. 'You're doing PE with me. In the gym. Now.'

We tried to explain further. Voices faltering. Eyes trying to avoid his but he just overrode us. We were doing PE. In the gym. In 60 seconds.

One or two of the boys were in a state of panic. They hadn't got any kit, they protested. That didn't matter, said Sackett. But what should they wear? they asked. That was their problem, he replied.

It was only the belated arrival of one of our art teachers – late, out of breath and in a paisley tie – that caused Sackett to back off. He listened to his colleague in silence. Smiled a wintry smile. And then, like a predatory animal prepared to wait for a better day, he slunk off.

There were plenty of other maniacs on the staff. One of the worst was Reddy, an assistant physics master who also helped Sackett on the rugger pitch. Reddy was a bespectacled and volatile little man with a thick neck and a large, bulbous nose. His hair was always cut savagely short and day after day he wore the same check sports jacket, badly fitting grey flannel trousers and highly polished brown shoes. He was always hitching up his trousers in class and when he took his jacket off and stood with his back to us, writing on the blackboard, we could see that his shirts seemed to have detachable lower arms that could be removed to make them short-sleeved in summer. And we could see that he wore string vests beneath his shirt and that the vests often had holes in them.

Reddy used to stride into the physics laboratory at the beginning of each lesson and immediately start dictating theorems at us loudly and chalking up details of an experiment on the board. Most of us didn't have the faintest idea what he was going on about but we knew that we had to copy down his words and imitate his procedures as he went along and then reproduce the details exactly in our homework that evening.

Reddy never bothered to explain what the point of the experiment was or why we might want to know about the specific heat of naphthalene or whether it would have any use or application in our adult lives. Like other great chunks of our grammar-school curriculum we were just meant to assimilate the facts and regurgitate them at a later date. Providing we did this correctly we were deemed to have learned something.

In between bouts of teaching and dictation Reddy would strut around the room deriding our cack-handed experiments and haranguing us on a variety of subjects. He had an obsession with what he called the 'A40 sheepskin jacket crowd' whom he seemed to think were uppity types looking down on hard-working schoolmasters like himself. His other targets were pretty much the same as the headmaster's: long hair, red socks, pop music and students. Especially long-haired, left-wing students attempting to disrupt South African rugby tours of Britain. Sackett and Reddy, like most serious sporting types in *Daily Telegraph*-reading south-east England, were ardent supporters of sporting links with John Vorster's Republic and they regarded men like Peter Hain, chief organiser of the 1969 Stop The Tour protest, as nothing less than a communist and traitor.

There were times when Reddy's tempers and fits of pique just seemed risibly funny but there were other days when the classroom positively shook and reverberated with the teacher's rages. An older, calmer physics master who had the adjoining laboratory would hear the bellowing through the connecting door, turn to his pupils and say, eyebrow raised, 'Ah! Modern teaching methods.'

Reddy was especially fond of describing to us the various punishments we were all sure to be in line for. 'I don't beat,' he said one morning, sounding like a rueful Wackford Squeers. 'But the head beats.' That cheered him up again. 'You should be beaten, Morgan. And you, Reid. And Haynes and Pell and Walters. And as for you, Allen . . . ' At this point he stopped in front of a small and particularly wretched boy who smelled of urine well into his teens and was especially bad at physics. 'If I have anything to do about it you *will* be beaten. You'll be beaten until the tears are running down your face and then you'll be beaten again . . . '

Sackett was the hard man, Reddy the chief maniac. Though in that department I should also give an honourable mention to an assistant chemistry master called Turner, who was known to the boys as Creepy. He was tall and thin with very short hair, protruding teeth and glasses and he did indeed creep around the laboratory corridors. On Friday afternoons he joined Rodney Vincent Fricker in army officer's uniform. And he had to be addressed formally, even if you weren't in the corps, as Major

Turner. These two imbecilic military types, the pompous fat man and the mutant thin man, could be seen ordering their teenage troops to do exciting things like crawl across the rugby pitches on their stomachs, before locating and capturing various trees, sheds, dustbins and other suspicious-looking outposts of communist influence.

By the time I was 13 the school cadet corps was no longer compulsory but there was no escaping maths or physics, at least not until the sixth form and no escape at all from a lot of dull and unimaginative teaching.

When I was in the third form at Judd the senior history master spent nearly every lesson either dictating notes or getting us to write out, word for word, pages of G.R. Elton's treatise on the Tudors and Stuarts. There was no question of us being encouraged to think for ourselves. The only changes to the routine would come when he would break off to lecture us on the near unimprovable perfection of the British Constitution in general and the Royal Family in particular.

The greater the enthusiasm for prescriptive teaching methods, then the greater it seems is the accompanying zeal for discipline. And certainly the idea that there is one, preferable model of youthful behaviour, and that with the right mixture of exhortation and punishment it can be imposed from above, was one of the principal tenets of my Judd School headmaster, Mr F.H. Taylor. Known to his pupils as Frank. Or just plain Wank.

CHAPTER ELEVEN

Mr Taylor was a small, plump man with slicked-back hair and glasses. He used to peer over the top of them to register disapproval. He was fond of the traditional long schoolmaster's gown and he always wore suits. Black pinstripe or tweed with flappingly wide trouser legs and sensible turn-ups.

Taylor had an exaggeratedly fruity and high-pitched voice and in his manner and tone he resembled a cross between Roy Jenkins and a pompous solicitor in a P.G. Wodehouse novel. We boys grew used to the headmaster's soft r's and musical delivery. He was continually lecturing us during school assemblies and he never tired of declaiming that one of the most important aspects of our time at Judd was learning how to be 'a good chap'.

A good chap always had 'a proper haircut' and 'a decent turnout'. He understood the importance of discipline, hard work and team spirit. He played up and played the game. He played lots of character-building team games. He was never smutty or base. He would give service to the nation or failing that at least display management potential with the South Eastern Gas Board. He would respect the Queen and salute the flag. He would never wear red socks. He would learn to take it on the chin or, more specifically, on the backside. And if he absorbed all of these lessons correctly his fellow citizens would immediately recognise him to be an Old Juddian and, indisputably, the right sort of chap.

Taylor himself had been to a public school in Dorset where, as he often used to remind us, he had to take a cold shower every day before breakfast. The headmaster was tremendously keen that Judd should resemble his idea of what a public school was like in all kinds of superficial ways from the house and prefectorial system to the disciplinary rituals and the obsession with team games. The predominant atmosphere was one of closely guarded philistinism. We were allowed to put on one school play a year but there wasn't much else in the way of creative expression. The art department was a joke. We had a debating society but although seditious conversations did sometimes take place there or in English and history lessons the ranks of prefects were nearly always drawn from A level scientists and rugby players.

A plaque on the wall of the main hall recorded the names of those boys who in the past had gone on to university. Pride of place was reserved for successful entrants to Oxford and Cambridge. The headmaster had been to Fitzwilliam College, Cambridge, and if you were the right kind of academic chap he would attempt to steer you in that direction. Yet for all his veneration of the oldest universities, Old Juddians were more likely to end up in accountancy or working for the Midland Bank than running the Foreign Office.

Judd was a direct grant grammar school and Taylor was devoted to our founders, the Skinners Company, who made up the majority of the governing body and provided the annual chairman of the board. The Skinners came down once a year on Governors' Day and we boys were all under strict instructions to 'stand and clap spontaneously' as they entered the hall. Anyone who didn't clap spontaneously would've been hauled off and caned spontaneously.

We could always tell when the Governors were coming because their arrival would be preceded by the distinctive aroma of brandy and cigars: a legacy of the good lunch they'd just enjoyed in the Rose and Crown on Tonbridge High Street. Most of the Skinners were rather portly looking men with sleek, brilliantined hair and red faces. It was customary that they should wear their traditional fur gowns but as Speech Day was always at the end of July many of them would soon be sweating profusely and one or two would look as if they were on the point of expiring from a heart attack.

We all stayed standing to sing 'Jerusalem' and then after a long and unctuous report from Taylor, the guest speaker would respond with an effusive tribute to the great, character-building qualities of the school. There were frequent references in the speeches to Conservative politicians who were always invoked as staunch supporters of the grammar-school ethos. In one memorable address in 1971 the Skinners' Secretary, J.S. Keith, informed us, 'I have spoken to the Secretary of State for Education, Mrs Thatcher, and she has assured me it will be comprehensive over her dead body.'

'That would be acceptable,' one or two of us muttered smugly, blissfully unaware that it was Thatcherism and not left-wing revolution that would one day inherit the Home Counties earth.

Mr Taylor often went up to see the Governors in London, sometimes travelling by train. One winter afternoon after school in 1969 I was at Tonbridge station with a friend waiting for our train back to Leigh, Penshurst and Edenbridge. We were sitting on a table in the waiting-room and smoking a cigarette when we saw a familiar pair of stout boots making their way down the steps from the upstairs ticket office. They were followed by the equally familiar baggy trousers, dark coat and bowler hat of our headmaster who was clearly about to embark first class for Charing Cross and Skinners Hall. We practically swallowed our fags as we dived for cover but Taylor walked straight past the window without even noticing us. He seemed to be lost in a private reverie of unblemished good chappery and had shut his eyes and ears to the rude impurities of the outside world.

The headmaster was always going on about the war and few weeks went by without him lecturing us at least once during our morning assemblies on the Dunkirk spirit. We were continually exhorted to admire the discipline of the Guards regiments who, so we were told, had practised their parade ground drill on the beaches of northern France even as the German air force buzzed overhead.

To us Dunkirk, an event that had happened nearly 30 years before, sounded more like an ignominious disaster than a heroic triumph. We could appreciate the bravery of the small boats going over to evacuate the troops but grew weary of having the backbone of the Guards officers endlessly compared to our deplorable lack of moral fibre. A characteristic which, it seemed, we mainly exhibited by our preference for long hair and red socks. The headmaster sometimes made it sound as if the Luftwaffe spent much of the Battle of Britain trying to spy on the enemy pilots' dress code. Any evidence of decadent red-sock wearers would presumably have been seized on as proof that British morale was snapping at last.

If the years between 1939 and '45 were Taylor's Golden Age then the late 1960s were emphatically the era when decadent and subversive tendencies stalked the land. Not long after Harold Wilson's second election victory in 1966 the head gave us a long and sombre warning about the threat posed to British society by what he called 'the suede shoes brigade and the tinned salmon merchants'. But more usually he would be damning and punishing us for the length of our hair.

There were interminable hair inspections at Judd, sometimes in the hall or in our classrooms, sometimes en masse outside in the covered playground where the whole school would be lined up as if on roll call at Alcatraz. At one point offenders were loaned two and sixpence by the deputy headmaster and despatched into town with orders to seek an immediate short back and sides. Half a crown merely bought you a butchering behind the railway station. Those of us more concerned about our appearance pocketed the school's cash and took a bus ride to Tunbridge Wells, where we spent our own money in the basement hairdressing salon of Benjamin Francis, men's outfitters in the Lower High Street. The two resident stylists, who both looked like Stevie Marriot in The Small Faces, got to know us well and were adept at manicuring our hair just enough to pass muster while leaving us extra flaps and bunches that could pop out from behind our ears on Friday nights.

If Taylor reviled long hair, his most damning comments were reserved for students. In that era it was axiomatic, at least in the minds of staunch conservatives like the headmaster, for the very word 'student' to be accompanied by hissing and booing. They were all automatically labelled 'long-haired layabouts'. And Taylor's especial *bête noir* was the London School of Economics, which had been in the news after two demonstrators threw a can of red paint over a South African diplomat. I thought it all sounded like good fun and couldn't wait to join in but Taylor regarded the place as beyond the pale. He seemed completely oblivious of the fact that it was one of the most high-powered academic institutions in Western Europe. In his perorations it was always transformed into a sink school for Juddian rejects. I was frequently being told that if I didn't mend my ways I 'might just as well leave here now and join the rest of the long-haired degenerates at the LSE'.

Frankly, I'd have been only too happy to oblige but it wasn't that easy. I had to survive seven years of secondary education first and avoid falling or being pulled up in the O and A level stakes. Schools like Judd with their emphasis on factual learning and note-taking were obsessed with examination results. Most teachers left little room for individual thought and expression and their pupils were just like the most inhibited members of the English class in *The Dead Poets' Society*. 'Should we take notes on this, sir? Will there be a test?'

Of course, as with Robin Williams at the fictional Welton College, there were one or two teachers who soared gloriously above the collective mediocrity of the rest. Truly inspirational figures who taught me, encouraged me and helped save me from expulsion or leaving school at 16. In that sense Judd offered precisely the lifeline my parents had hoped for. A way out. A means of escape, ironically, from the very world that the headmaster and the Governors were so keen to promote.

The most inspiring figure of my first few years was a young history teacher called Mike Chester. He brought potentially dry subjects to life brilliantly, unfolding events like the Roman Invasion of Britain and the Norman Conquest as if they were one big, bloody and epic adventure story, allowing us to relish every detail of the battles, the intrigue, the violence and the sex.

In 1967 Chester was allowed to produce the school play and daringly chose Marlowe's *Dr Faustus*. Even if I didn't understand every word of the antique speech I could sense that there was something grippingly seditious about the story of a literate, questing man prepared to risk everything, including his mortal soul, for such carnal, temporal pleasures as a glimpse of Helen of Troy. To me, this kind of thing was way beyond F.H. Taylor's world view. Unfortunately he clearly thought so too and, frustrated by constant clashes with the headmaster and the school's overall stuffiness, Chester – who'd even gone so far as to grow a beard – left Judd a year later and emigrated to Australia.

D.R. Gibling, an assistant English master known to everyone as Dan, was never a staff-room leader or head of department. Few boys really appreciated him. He'd been brutally treated in a Japanese prisoner-of-war camp, though, unlike Taylor, he rarely mentioned the war and never excoriated our generation for any lack of military discipline. His experiences had left him physically and, I suspect, mentally damaged, the most obvious signs being various nervous tics and gestures that drew the laughter and ridicule of his classes. The more they mocked him the more he lost his temper, usually to no avail, but I found him a kindly and fundamentally decent man who loved books, especially poetry, and who, like Chester, possessed views well to the left of the headmaster.

The teacher who had the most influence on me, especially in the sixth form, was called Brian Mitchell and he was the head of English. A serious man in his mid-40s, Mitchell seemed to carry with him an air of resigned disappointment, as if life hadn't quite worked out in the way he'd hoped. He was another left-winger and his classroom was always a forum for debate and dissent, but Mitchell's positions were complex and he was quick to challenge our own rather shallow and half-baked views. He was a keen advocate of athletics and cross-country running and issued sober warnings about the damage he thought adolescents were doing to themselves with drink, drugs and cigarettes.

Regardless of his puritanical streak, Mitchell was a first-class teacher with a passionate love of his subject and a fierce determination to make us understand the difference between objective and subjective arguments. He encouraged us to dismiss emotive rhetoric – including his own – and showed us how to order our thoughts in speech and on paper in a coherent and articulate manner.

Mitchell could get excited about all the set texts he had to teach but he loved Shakespeare in general and *Hamlet* in particular, the Metaphysical Poets such as Donne, Herbert and Marvell, and Siegfried Sassoon's gentle but deeply affecting *Memoirs of a Foxhunting Man* and *Memoirs of an Infantry Officer*, autobiographical accounts that had their origins in the same west Kent countryside that we were all growing up in.

Mitchell was a hard marker and he used praise more sparingly than Dan. He made me realise that if I really loved English literature and wanted to study it properly and in depth I would have to apply myself. He always encouraged me to think of going to university and was instrumental in persuading me to apply to Oxford. Yet, like a lot of other teachers, friends and allies, I think he often despaired of my capacity for getting into trouble and my apparent inability or just stubborn refusal to master any subject other than the two or three I was really interested in.

Throughout my first year at Judd, anxious to conform to the Stakhanovite ethos, I'd tried frantically to do well at everything, running on the spot like a dutiful schoolboy. It was no fun at all. At the end of the first term Sackett read out our form positions in front of the whole class. We all looked around nervously, waiting to hear our name and number called. There were 32 boys in all and when Sackett, wearing his usual thin smile, announced, 'Ellison. Thirty-second,' we all stared pityingly at this unfortunate creature who tried to keep his eyes from meeting ours. Some of the swots in the top three or four places smirked obnoxiously at their good fortune and even more so at the plight of others. It was as if they had just ascended to the ranks of the elect, the saints on earth, whereas Ellison and his like had joined the company of the damned and could no longer be spoken to by daylight.

I came top in the English and history exams and in the bottom half-dozen in all science subjects, so my overall form position in the summer of 1966 was somewhere around halfway, or 16th. By the second summer I'd slipped into the bottom 10. Subjects like maths and physics remained a mystery to me. If you asked a man like Reddy to slow down or repeat himself because you couldn't understand what he was saying, he just shouted at you. If you didn't ask and you got it wrong he'd shout even louder. So why bother trying?

In the autumn of 1967 our year was split into three streams and I found myself in what was supposed to be the lowest tier. I didn't mind a bit. It was a lot more congenial than being bracketed with the informers and goodie-goodies in the top set. I think our class contained the biggest proportion of slackers and troublemakers in the entire school. I loved it and as the Summer of Love gave way to 1968, the year of revolution, I started consciously – perhaps it should be self-consciously – seeking out bad influences and embracing every strain of rebellion against the authorities.

There were two sets of bad company you could choose to rebel with at Judd and in Tonbridge and Tunbridge Wells: the hippies and the lads. The latter were livelier and up until the sixth form they were often more fun but the hippies were in the majority. This was the late '60s after all. The whole hippy look, not just the long hair but the tie-dyed shirts and firemen's jackets, the greatcoats, kaftans, flowers, bells and cheap joss stick smell of it all could always be relied upon to enrage Messrs Sackett, Reddy and F.H. Taylor.

Yet in the more sophisticated and not so disgusted purlieus of Tunbridge Wells, handsome residential streets like Broadwater Down and Boyne Park, there were one or two splendidly liberal and slightly debauched families (or so they would have had you think) whose responses were more tolerant. These were households where Rosé was drunk at 11 in the morning, where bedroom walls were painted purple and where copies of *Nova* were left lying around in the loo. The men had suave accents and wore jeans and pink shirts at the weekends. Some of them had jobs in the City or advertising. Some laid claim to an artistic temperament and camped about like Laurence Olivier, only later to be revealed as something like the catering manager at the Adelaine Genee Theatre in East Grinstead. These were men who were theoretically entirely in favour of the concept of free love but who spluttered apoplectically and reached for the horsewhip if there was any chance that their gorgeous nubile daughters, bosoms fallings out of their Indian cotton shirts, might actually be at it.

Fortunately the mothers of these confident smoky-eyed 15 and 16 year olds were often rather husky, sexy women who were themselves busy having affairs – and suicide attempts – and who had introduced their daughters to the pill and were prepared to let their teenage boyfriends stay all night at weekends. The girls – and their mothers – wore black eye make-up, Biba dresses and boots, and Bonnie Parker berets, and swooned adoringly over poetic, long-haired boys whose parents and teachers didn't understand them.

Further afield in stockbroker Sevenoaks parents were altogether more tricky. Returning to their mock-Tudor fastness with a blonde girlfriend in tow after a certain hour was to be greeted by a stern paterfamilias in a dressing-gown, armed with a golf club and enquiring, 'Is it just me? Or is it what I represent?'

Hippy girls and boys were expected to go on to university or art school or just to drop out. The lads, who came from places like Tonbridge and Paddock Wood, had different expectations.

The lads were generally the most working-class boys in the school with fathers who were skilled craftsmen or mechanics or men who worked on the railways. And whereas middle-class mothers looked after the home, the lads' mothers all had full- or part-time jobs. Most of the lads wanted to leave school at 16 and most of their parents encouraged them believing, as my father's mother had done in the early '30s, that gainful employment rather than higher education should be the priority for their adolescent sons.

F.H. Taylor colluded disgracefully with these restrictive horizons. If Judd's hippies and refuseniks were 'long-haired layabouts', then in Taylor's mind the lads were all 'hooligans and troublemakers'. He could presumably feel all that boyish testosterone swirling around and he wanted to get shot of it as quickly as possible. It was a criminal waste of the lads' potential. The best of them were bright, quick-witted boys with an ability to sum things up succinctly and directly, and with none of the vapid clichés of hippiedom. Judd, with its rigid attitudes and unbending teaching methods, left their intellectual abilities largely untapped.

In the summer of their O level year Taylor would sometimes 'intercede personally' to get one of the lads a position as a junior office boy with a London-based firm with Skinners Company connections like Wiggins Teape or Tate & Lyle. Others were encouraged to join the army or the merchant navy. Few of them stayed on to do A levels.

In the 1960s the lads and their families supported Harold Wilson. I've no doubt that ten years later many of them voted for Margaret Thatcher and if they'd left grammar school in 1980 or 1985 as opposed to 1970, I suppose they might have been part of the brash, big-bang takeover of the City. Mr Taylor could hardly have guessed that the lads and their type would one day end up storming Threadneedle Street but I like to think that one or two of them, or their sons and daughters, made it big-time in the end. And livened up the suffocating atmosphere of the first-class carriages on the commuter trains to Cannon Street and Charing

Cross with the splash of bubbly and the trilling of mobile phones.

Some of the lads had older brothers who'd been Mods in 1964 and '65 and like them had short, sharp haircuts and some still rode around on Vespas, wearing a Parka or a furry-collared car coat. The only mainstream rock band they liked was The Who. Otherwise their musical tastes were all soul and Tamla Motown.

The lads were hot at picking up girls – more confident and less fumbling than the hippies – and they went out on Friday and Saturday nights to dances and discos at places like the Teen and Twenty Club down Barden Park Road behind Tonbridge public library. The lads wore stay-pressed trousers and Ben Sherman shirts with button-down collars, and the more dapper lads, the ones with evening and weekend jobs, even owned a suit, a sartorial item that seemed comically irrelevant from the hippy perspective.

The lads walked around bow-legged with their feet pointing out and hands in their pockets or their thumbs in their waistband. They smoked Three Castles and Embassy Gold Leaf and they danced to The Temptations and the Isley Brothers and Marvin Gaye.

The lads' girlfriends, who had suits of their own, chewed gum and blew fag smoke over the boys' shoulders. They were pretty but hard and for most of them the adventurous and experimenting part of their lives would not last long, as they were destined for marriage and a family before they were 21. In 1968 and '69 though, on their 15- and 16-year-old Friday and Saturday nights out, they dressed up and wore perfume and smooched to 'This Old Heart of Mine' and 'I Heard It Through The Grapevine'. Afterwards they and their paramours went outside and later that night or at school the following Monday the lads would boast of how far they'd gone up against the wall or in the Remembrance Gardens. The sound of Edwin Starr still booming out from the first-floor dance hall, as the clouds of cigarette smoke and the smell of cheap scent drifted towards the empty, sodium arc-lit platforms of nearby Tonbridge station.

One or two of the lads went looking for trouble and

excitement beyond Tonbridge and as far away as exotic destinations like Maidstone, and even to a ska and blue beat bar in Lewisham, where a mate of a lad was mates with a fabulously cool West Indian by the name of Flash Roach. The Flash wore signet rings on each hand and sold uppers and downers to the lads and dope to the hippies.

Roach was once involved in a knife fight with another dealer called Lloyd. Roach took a knife wound and his mate took his car coat, eagerly sought after by the police, and gave it to one of our lads who hid this incriminating item of evidence in his locker in the changing-room of the sedate Judd School. Some of us were allowed in to see it at break times. The atmosphere charged with excitement and danger as the lads laid hands on Roach's white sheepskin, the lining stained deep red. F.H. Taylor would surely have had a seizure if he'd seen us.

Some of the lads were enthusiastic punters. The hippies were generally too mellow for something as full-blooded as betting and racing but the lads were excited by odds and gambling and one of them in particular was a dedicated follower of Lester Piggott. In the summer of 1968 we got what money we could on Lester's mount Sir Ivor in the Derby. The price was short but we didn't care. The Long Fellow produced one of the most sublimely artistic displays in racing history, unleashing the favourite with a thrilling winning run inside the final furlong.

We backed Lester again on Nijinsky in 1970. He too was trained by Vincent O'Brien and he too was an American-bred colt. Handsome, highly strung and fast. They said the two French challengers Gyr and Stintino could each be a champion. Lester gave both of them a start. You can praise courage and stamina in a horse but the most important of all qualities, especially on the flat, is speed. Nijinsky had speed. Lester knew he had it and they were the most exciting flat-racing combination I've ever seen.

The Turf had remained as much a private passion for me as it had been during my time at primary school. And betting on racehorses now seemed to be an enjoyable if modest way of rebelling against Judd's stifling orthodoxy. But in November 1968, a wager I placed on the Mackeson Gold Cup at Cheltenham, the first big steeplechase of the winter, landed me in what Mr Taylor described as 'very hot water indeed'. And set in motion a year-long chain of events that very nearly ended my grammar-school career.

CHAPTER TWELVE

One of the most unpopular punishments at Judd was a Master's Detention which obliged you to go into school on a Saturday morning in full uniform. You and your fellow detainees would sit in a half-empty classroom and toil away at some tedious piece of written work for one, two or sometimes even three hours.

The detentions were supervised by members of staff who were themselves on a punishment rota. Most of them disliked being there as much as the boys did, though, of course, disciplinarians like Reddy made the most of things, issuing ferocious commands to keep silent at all times and always on the lookout for an opportunity to add on more hours for some minor infringement or other.

Saturday Club, as the boys called it, ruined one of the greatest pleasures of the weekend: the Saturday morning lie-in, followed, in my case, by a leisurely perusal of the runners, riders and form for that afternoon's televised racing. It was not advisable to be late for a detention. If somebody like Sackett or Reddy was in charge, you ran the risk of being hauled back again the following week. So if I was in detention and there was any question of the trains not running on time, I'd have to get up even earlier than usual and catch the 8:00 to Tonbridge as opposed to the 8:30.

The school had another way of ruining your weekend in that

they scheduled nearly all sporting fixtures on a Saturday afternoon. They too had to be attended in full school uniform and if it was an away match in a neighbouring county, there was a good chance that a large part of the day would be knocked out.

One November Saturday in 1968, when I was 14 years old, I managed an unwelcome double. I had a detention, handed down by Reddy if I remember, for being caught smoking during the lunch hour. Then in the afternoon I had to go off to a cross-country running match against Brighton College. I absolutely loathed cross-country with all its dour, spartan, pain-is-good-for-you overtones (even now the sight of a virtuously suffering jogger makes me want to grab a packet of Marlboro Reds, light up several of them at once and blow smoke into their eyes) but I had briefly ended up in the team simply because I did track running – 100 metres, 200 metres, as short a distance as possible – in the summer.

There would be no time to go home between the detention ending and the Judd minibus departing for the south coast. So that morning I set off from our house in near darkness, lugging my running kit in one bag and schoolwork in another. The detention was supervised by a science master called Plumb, who lived with his mother in Tunbridge Wells. His laboratory was one of the oldest and dingiest in the school and half a dozen of us sat there yawning in poor light and writing out our impositions, surrounded by specimen jars filled with preserved slices of dissected squirrel, catfish and rat.

Shortly after 11 we were released and a friend and I wandered down into the town to have a coffee in the Scandinavia, a popular Saturday Club venue that had a good jukebox and tolerated under-age smoking. Before going back up to school I went into a betting office situated, as they were in those days, not in the full, respectable glare of the High Street but down a side street near the station. The shop (which was pulled down years ago to make way for a supermarket development) was a companionable gambling enclave. There was only an audio commentary and just a few stools to sit on but the pages of the *Sporting Life* were pinned up around the wall and nobody ever asked you to move on in a hurry.

The highlight that Saturday was the two-and-a-half-mile Mackeson Gold Cup, which, frustratingly, was live on the BBC. It was the first big race of the season and the favourite was a horse called Charlie Worcester from the Ryan Price stable. I fancied Jupiter Boy, whose trainer Fred Rimell had won the 1961 Grand National with Nicolaus Silver and who, along with his wife Mercy, was to become one of the great Cheltenham Festival specialists. I had some money on me that I'd been given by Gilbert Butcher for a winner the previous week, so I had ten shillings each way on Jupiter Boy. Then, after looking at the form for the other races for a while longer, I left the shop and walked back up to the school.

Plumb was also in charge of the intermediate cross-country team and it took about an hour and a half for him to drive us down to Brighton. The college, a bleak penitential-looking private academy, was up near Kemptown not far from the racecourse. We got changed in the school changing-rooms with Plumb, another master with a penchant for glimpses of half-naked adolescents, hanging around voyeuristically in the background. Then we were driven out to a bare and miserably exposed point high up on the Downs by the Devil's Dyke road. The course took us along a ridge heading west, parallel with the sea, then dropped down into a valley before climbing up again steeply past a golf course and rejoining the track we'd set out on.

It was a bitterly cold afternoon and by the time the race got underway the wind was whipping in off the Channel, lashing our bare legs and splattering snot out of our noses and onto our cheeks. Staggering back up the hill past the golf course I was suddenly aware of Plumb, wrapped up in an overcoat and scarf and standing by a car. 'Come along, Reid,' he shouted idiotically. 'Sprint. Sprint for home.' Had I not been on the point of expiring from hypothermia, I would gladly have fallen upon him, shaken him violently by the throat and flung him over the nearest ravine.

When the race was over Plumb kept us standing about a bit longer while he called for three cheers for the opposing team. Then we were driven back to the college in the fading light. We were allowed to de-freeze in a hot shower and then awarded the luxury of a cup of hot soup and a bread roll.

On the journey back to Tonbridge in the November dark, a friend switched on his transistor radio and we listened to the football results on *Sports Report* and then to the racing results. To my unconcealed joy, I discovered that Jupiter Boy had won the Mackeson and at a starting price of 9–1, several points shorter than the odds I'd been given. I felt a warm glow spreading up from my toes. I was over £6 richer. There were more than four months of top-quality jump racing ahead. And this interminable day was nearly over.

The following Monday, school resumed in what seemed to be its usual turgid fashion. But after break I was sent for by the headmaster. Taylor was in a thunderous mood. He informed me that on Saturday morning I had been 'observed entering the offices of a turf accountant . . . in school uniform'. There was apparently no point in me denying it. Some insufferable busy-body of a maths master, who clearly had nothing better to do on Saturday mornings than bicycle around Tonbridge spying on errant Juddians, had seen me go in. And had waited for me to come out. And had then felt obliged to report his findings to the head.

It was not the worst crime in Judd school history you might have thought, but Taylor's expression said otherwise. And in words that must have been borrowed from Terry Thomas, he informed me my offence was so heinous that there was only one suitable punishment – I should have to have 'a jolly good thrashing'.

The headmaster was an enthusiastic thrasher. On his afternoons off he kept his hand in by flogging the fairways at nearby Lamberhurst golf course. He seemed to attach a sort of spiritual dimension to the administration of justice, as if we were all characters in some 1950s film about Borstal and delinquency and would one day look back from the vantage point of mature adulthood and agree it was the headmaster's firm measures that had put us on the path to a sober and responsible life. He didn't quite go so far as to add that we'd probably end up sending him a Christmas card every year but I've no doubt his sentiments tended that way.

Taylor's executions weren't always carried out immediately. There was sometimes a delay of two or three days to allow for a period of suitably baleful contemplation. But then the awful summons would finally come and you'd have to walk through the hall and the dining-room and along the corridor to the headmaster's study. There used to be a bulb over the door rather like the blue lamp outside a police station. If the light was on you had to wait outside on the bench. If it was off you had to knock and at the cry of 'Enter' step inside to doom.

Many years later I read an account by Jeffrey Bernard of a similar beating he received at Pangbourne Naval College after being caught laying bets to other boys. He concluded that the pleasures of racing and gambling must be comparable to cigarettes, alcohol and sex because they were the only other 'vices' that encouraged such savage reprisals from arterio-sclerotic adults. I felt much the same but this being the late '60s, the era of *If* and the student riots in France, I decided that hedonism alone was not enough. There would have to be a calculated show of defiance against the authorities.

Mr Taylor and his counterpart at Tonbridge School actually went to see *If* together. They staged a joint walk-out halfway through, helpfully informing a reporter from the local paper that the film was 'tripe'. Their review did wonders for ticket sales, with schoolkids flocking from all around the area, and we put it about that they were on a percentage from the manager of the Ritz cinema.

My own rebellion ranged from no doubt rather embarrassing defences of pupils' liberties and civil rights in response to various acts of staff-room 'fascism', to the standard battles over hair and red socks, to low-grade acts of guerrilla warfare conducted with laddish mates at the expense of selected prefects. On one occasion we threw a bucket of water and a mop down some stairs and over the head of the particularly officious head boy. Such acts of 'mindless vandalism', as the headmaster called them, were always more enjoyable than political speeches, though in Taylor's view the possession of *Oz*, the *International Times* and the *Little Red School Book* were equally serious when calculating an ascending scale of villainy.

It all came to a head in November 1969, a year after the Jupiter Boy saga. I got into a public row with a young classics teacher who clearly felt that his credibility was on the line. At the time I had images of Malcolm McDowell machine-gunning the guests at Speech Day, but it wasn't quite that heroic and afterwards I felt rather ashamed to have behaved so obnoxiously.

I was reported to Taylor as usual and informed that I would have to see him on a Saturday morning after I had finished a rehearsal for the school play. At midday I reluctantly made my way back to the bench in the corridor. The light was off. I knocked. There was no reply. I tried the handle. The room was empty. I hung around for ten minutes but there was still no sign of the headmaster.

I wanted to get back home as quickly as possible to watch *Grandstand*. It was, after all, the Hennessy Gold Cup at Newbury, an event of even greater importance than the Mackeson. All right, I thought. Maybe this is my lucky day. Maybe he's forgotten. And I slipped out of the office door and walked off down the service drive and down the hill to the station. Spanish Steps won the Hennessy at 7–1. My selection, Lord Jim, finished third at 17–2.

The following Monday I arrived back at school with that slightly sinking feeling that tells you trouble is in store. For the first hour or so it was just the normal boring routine. Then, shortly before midday, the lesson I was in was interrupted by the deputy headmaster arriving like an arresting officer to inform me, in front of the whole class, that the headmaster wanted to see me immediately.

Taylor was grave. I had ignored his summons. I tried to explain but excuses were futile. He claimed to be appalled by the classics master incident. But there were to be no thrashings this time. I was presumably too old or just too big. Instead, he solemnly informed me, he would be writing to my parents and consulting with the Governors and as a result of those discussions I might well be expelled from the Judd School.

Leaving Taylor's office I knew I ought to be jubilant. I'd been trying my best to get thrown out for the last year and a half but, hovering on my own on the edges of the playing field, I felt not so much gleeful as guilty. I'd really gone and done it. But what about my parents? How worried and disappointed they'd be. And how could I possibly explain to them what had happened?

I decided I'd have to get to them before Taylor did. There was no alternative to confessing, with as much spin on things as possible, that evening. It wasn't the easiest suppertime I'd ever experienced but I did a good job of projecting myself as the victim of tyrannical oppression and, to my relief, my mother was sympathetic while my father was calm and reasonable. He told me he'd respond to Taylor's letter when it came and that whatever the 'difficulty' was, he was sure it could all be sorted out. I wasn't so confident. I longed to leave Judd and I was pretty certain Taylor was eager to grant me my wish. But what would that do to my father, who'd been forced to leave school at 16, and had always hoped his younger son would escape the restrictive horizons that had limited his life?

Taylor's letter duly arrived and for once, and to my great surprise, my father, normally the most shy and retiring of men, announced that he would go and see the headmaster on his own. When the day of his visit came I tried to block it out and would happily have removed myself from the scenario altogether. But mid-morning, as I was on my way from one classroom in the main building to another uncomfortably close to Taylor's study, I saw my father walking in through the school gates in his British Warm overcoat and his brown trilby hat. I watched him going through the green front door of the office past the photographs of past members of the school rugby and cricket teams. He didn't see me but in a very real sense he was going in to bat on my behalf and I knew that the encounter had the potential to be distinctly uncomfortable for him.

Taylor, the ex-public school man with his golf club membership and his cravats at the weekend, would be all charm on the surface. But there could be a poisonously patronising side to F. H. T., an insinuating manner not so far removed from my aunt's comment about Alex being 'almost a gentleman'. My father would be courteous, as when dealing with an overbearing customer in the shop on Saturdays, but I feared it wouldn't be easy for the carpet-salesman to challenge the headmaster's assertions. But then, as I realised later, I'd seriously underestimated him. At the age of 15 I may've imagined I was already cleverer than he was but there were things he knew which I didn't begin to understand.

My father's father, also Alexander Reid, was a Scotsman. One of five sons of a factor or farm manager from a village near Invergordon, north of Inverness. One of Alexander's brothers was a chemist in Wick. Another was a schoolteacher while a third, great-uncle Alec, had a farm at Torrachilty near Muir of Ord. He was a strict Presbyterian. My mother was evacuated there from Kent with my older brother in 1942 but she found it a dour home. The English newspapers were frowned upon on Sundays, when everyone was expected to go to church twice, and then the local minister came round for more prayers and sandwiches in the evening.

Some men rebelled. Another of Alexander's brothers worked in a whisky distillery. He was a romantic but melancholy man and he drank heavily. One night he was knocked down and killed by a train while walking back along the railway line from Dingwall to Garve. He was paralytic at the time.

Alexander was fascinated by machinery and he loved taking apart bicycles and wireless sets. As a boy he saw a Rolls Royce Silver Cloud driven through Invergordon by a local laird who'd had it shipped up from England. A few years later the teenager went south to be an apprentice in the Rolls Royce factory in Derby. When he left there he became a chauffeur.

For more than 25 years my grandfather worked for a man called Lord Ebbisham, who owned Fairmile, a large house with grounds and a kitchen garden near Esher, not far from Sandown Park racecourse. There Alexander met his future wife, Lily Sawyer. She was a chambermaid. They had three sons, George, Alex and Ian, and they lived in a street called Progress Villas in Ashtead.

Alexander survived four years in the Royal Artillery in the First World War returning, unlike many veterans, to a home and a secure job. While his own boys were growing up they often played with Lord Ebbisham's son, Sandy, whose thrice-yearly returns to his boarding school were conducted by my grandfather, doing his best to be cheerful, while Sandy sat alone and in tears, in the vast back seat of his father's Packard.

The Ebbishams spent August at their summer house on the Isle of Wight and the chauffeur's family went too. A cottage was rented for them in Seaview. My father always remembered the drives down to Portsmouth harbour, he and his brothers rolling around in the same fabulously upholstered motor in which their father had driven His Lordship the day before.

The boys went to Tiffins School, which was eventually to become a grammar school not unlike Judd. Alex was thought capable of passing the school leaving certificate but his mother, mindful of the onset of the Depression, felt her sons had no business 'idling around' in education beyond a certain point. So when he was 16 she took him out of school and told him he was to become an apprentice carpet-fitter, a choice arrived at for no better reason than that he was 'good with his hands' and somebody knew someone at Bentalls in Kingston who'd said they'd take him on.

From that 16-year-old summer in 1931 to this November 1969, my father had been working five-and-a-half-day weeks, 49 weeks of the year, with only the war years intervening. In 1938, the year of the Czechoslovakia crisis and the Munich Agreement, he'd joined the territorial army (enlisting, out of respect for his family, in the London Scottish) and the following September he was one of the first to be called up.

In the autumn of 1940, having lived through the Dunkirk debacle, the regiment was stationed near Edenbridge, where the 18-year-old Paula Tanner was working, like other young women of the parish, in an outdoor refreshment tent that had been set up for visiting servicemen. Alex came into the canteen one day in his kilt and his glengarry. He was a handsome man with his blue eyes and his black hair and moustache and the couple met and fell passionately in love. They were married six months later in the teeth of my grandmother's disapproval. The London Scotsman was not only not quite a gentleman, he was also an NCO and not an officer.

Alex survived both the war and a near-fatal car crash when he was on leave in 1943. His younger bother Ian was less fortunate. He was shot down and killed in a Lancaster Bomber over Cambrai, northern France. He was 21 years old.

At least my father, like his father before him, had a job to go back to. He worked hard through the austerity years and in the early '50s my parents bought their house in Leigh. They slaved to pay a mortgage and to bring up three children. My older brother and my sister were both born during the war. I was a post-war baby, though not too late to be issued with a ration book. In common with many others of my generation I think I was partly living out the hopes and expectations of my parents, whose own lives had been curtailed in ways I'd never fully comprehend. Most of my father's closest friends – young, vital men in their early 20s – had been killed on the beaches at Anzio. Shot to pieces as they came off the landing craft. Now the post-war meritocracy, part of the settlement they'd died for, offered me the prospect of an unimaginably different life. And my father wasn't about to let me fall or drop out before I'd even taken my O levels.

As my father explained to me later that evening, Taylor presented the case for the prosecution 'more in sorrow than in anger'. Naturally. But it was clear that as far as the headmaster was concerned a verdict of guilty leading to expulsion (or exclusion as it would be called in today's euphemistic jargon) was preordained. Taylor wheeled out the hapless classics master, who, according to my father, was shaking. 'You picked the wrong one there, J,' he said to me later. My father apologised to him graciously on my behalf. The classics master responded by offering a generous tribute to my academic potential, one which clearly irritated the headmaster, and then left the room. After he'd gone Taylor broadened his indictment. He brought up the incident with the bucket of water and several others like it. My father said his older brother George had done far worse when he was 15. Taylor, his air of superiority slightly dented, fumed about appearance and turn-out. My father quietly denounced a regime where 'young people' were labelled as degenerates and layabouts simply because of the length of their hair. 'Touché, Mr Reid,' said F.H.T. smarmily. 'Touché.'

The mood was subtly changing. My father suggested that these 'problems' would all settle down once everyone was concentrating on O and A level results and university applications. Appealing to Taylor's vanity, to his yearning for more names on that honours board in the hall, was the turning point. The headmaster insisted that I would have to write a letter of apology to the classics master and there would be yet another Saturday morning detention. But as long as I agreed to 'play the game' all talk of expulsion would be lifted. And there might even be fewer references to hair and red socks.

When I heard about this settlement that evening I wasn't sure if I should be grateful or indignant. It felt as if I'd given in completely and was now a prisoner of the authorities. But my wise father, who'd learned how to deal with bullies and martinets in the army, counselled me to keep my head down, to be a little less visible and to play it long. 'In a few years' time,' he said, 'you'll have got what you need from school. And then you'll never have to deal with these people again.'

So began a near two-year period of doing my duplicitous best to be if not a model pupil, at least a relatively taciturn and inconspicuous one. Other than in English and history lessons that is.

O levels came and went in the summer of 1970 and I performed pretty much as expected, getting As in the things I liked and failing all the rest. England's World Cup campaign in Mexico and Lester and Nijinsky at Epsom Downs were a lot more compelling than exams.

At the end of the summer term Mr Taylor retired. On Governors' Day there were interminable speeches extolling his record and qualities, attributes 'recognised and admired by successive generations of school boys', according to a Skinners Company spokesman. On the final day we were all organised into another one of those memorable Juddian displays of Soviet-style spontaneity. The head boy Edmeades, a future police inspector, called for three cheers for Mr T. and then on cue we all stood to applaud his exit from the hall. As he left he had tears in his eyes. Perhaps he'd caught a last, infuriating glimpse of red socks in the audience and feared for his legacy.

He needn't have worried.

CHAPTER THIRTEEN

There had been some suggestions locally that the Skinners Company might decide that Taylor's retirement, coinciding as it did with the onset of a new decade, was the ideal moment for the school to embrace a less conservative and more forward-looking approach. Not a bit of it. The Governors, it seemed, shared F.H.T.'s view that the scourge of the '60s, rebellious and degenerate behaviour, had to be expunged from Judd's joyless corridors. Mr Taylor had, perhaps, been too old and too soft to deal effectively with the matter. But his replacement was to be a very hard case indeed.

E.P. Riddle, Christian name Eric, was a tall, thin, humourless man in his late 40s. He had a long, red nose and was quickly nicknamed Peen, as in penis, by the boys. Where Taylor had been a Macmillanesque High Tory, Riddle was a sort of Heathite technocrat. A brisk administrator bereft of imagination. His university degree had been in economics but he did little teaching at Judd. He was too busy being a policeman. He began by observing suspects then, halfway through his second term, he launched into a reign of terror designed, in classic manner, to make a few examples *pour encourager les autres*.

At the high point of the drama three boys were expelled from the upper sixth for displaying 'a consistent and unacceptable anti-social attitude'. The whole school was summoned to an assembly in the middle of the afternoon to hear the news. Liberals like Mitchell winced but fellow hard-liners like Sackett and Reddy looked on approvingly. Riddle treated us to a cliché-laden speech about 'rotten apples' and 'cracking down' and I realised how lucky I was he hadn't been in charge the year before.

For a day or two there was frantic speculation that more expulsions would follow. Boys looked around nervously as they moved from classroom to classroom and a mood of fear and uncertainty gripped the whole dismal institution.

Spying and grassing up malcontents was positively encouraged by our new headmaster. Prefects, he declared, should not tolerate dissent. And even quite trivial offences might earn a trip to his study for what he described enthusiastically as 'whacking on the backside'. No change from F.H. Taylor's Greyfriars regime there, then.

As a reward for dissembling and biting my tongue I was told I was to be made a monitor, which was a sort of joke status that stopped some way short of being a full prefect. Like a prisoner looking for the cushiest option, I managed to get assigned to the library, which meant I could spend even more time reading books than I did already, and kept me out of the way of Riddle and his plain-clothes team.

I loved A level history and English. Even more so I loved the special English lessons with Mitchell and Dan. These were designed to prepare me and a friend for the Oxbridge entrance exam, which it had been decided I would sit in November 1971, rather than wait until I'd taken my A levels the following year.

At the time the whole concept of applying to Oxford seemed more Brian Mitchell's and my parents' idea than my own. I could tell that one or two staff members didn't think I should even have been entered, given that I'd only passed five O levels. Judd, after all, was a school that spent inordinate amounts of time lording the virtues of boys who obediently consumed and digested enough facts to pass more like ten or twelve.

But then, as I was about to discover, the Oxford entrance exam was very different to a typical O and A level memory test. In the English literature paper there would be three hours to answer just three questions on whomsoever you pleased from Chaucer to Keats and Dylan Thomas, and from Shakespeare to Oscar Wilde. The general paper was even better and gave you three hours to write just two essays chosen from a huge range of topical and polemic issues from the Vietnam War to Republicanism and the monarchy and from the history of the Commonwealth to surrealist art. The aim was not just to assess your ability to regurgitate spoon-fed knowledge. It was positively encouraging you to be bold, be imaginative, to construct a coherent argument, yes, but also – heresy in Juddian eyes – to think for yourself.

That was the target but as the first half of 1971 rumbled along, progress seemed painfully slow and my release date still a long way off. I was compelled to take a few more O levels, including religious education, to improve my tally. I kept my hair as short as I could bear and did my best to stay out of trouble.

On the racetrack the Irish chaser L'Escargot, carrying the same colours that Lester had worn on Sir Ivor in the 1968 Derby, won the Cheltenham Gold Cup for the second year running. L'Escargot was a wonderful horse trained by Dan Moore and ridden by his son-in-law Tommy Carberry. He went on to be third and second to Red Rum in successive Grand Nationals and then to finally win the Aintree race in 1975. And up until Best Mate's second Gold Cup victory in March 2003 he was the only horse since Arkle to have won the race twice. There could be no skiving off school that spring though. I had to dash out of the gates at 3.40 p.m. and run down the hill and watch the race unfold without sound through the windows of Radio Rentals on Tonbridge High Street. I hadn't had a bet. I was doing my best to conform and avoid all temptation but conforming wasn't always easy.

Each day at Tonbridge station I saw many of the boys who'd left Judd at 16 to take their A levels at West Kent College on the outskirts of Tunbridge Wells. They seemed to have achieved ultimate freedom. They were the boys of summer in their ruin. They could wear their own clothes and smoke and grow their hair as long as they wanted and everybody claimed that at college the lessons weren't even compulsory.

Judd schoolmasters implied darkly that West Kent was just a haven for drop-outs and that no reputable A level or career progress could be made from that address. I wasn't so sure at the time, though perhaps in some underlying way – and I hate to admit it – they had a point. 'College' was a relatively small and undemanding world and once settled in it was easy to get stuck.

As a 16 year old I envied the 'drop-outs' their hours spent in Coffee Corner opposite the central station, stubbing out fags in glass saucers and then drifting up to the Grove – Tunbridge Wells' bohemia – for a joint in somebody's one-room flat. But they were still in the same place two or three years later and some of them were still there, or in the pub across the road, 10 or 15 years after that. Fattening now in early middle age. In jackets and ties. Working for an estate agent or the local council. Popping into the pub for a lunchtime pint and a pie and in some cases even playing for the Old Juddian rugby club at weekends. Those oft talked about trips to Big Sur and Marrakesh never quite coming off and a collection of old Hendrix and Cream LPs their only remaining link to a time when they were rebels. For them, their mid to late teens really were the best years of their lives.

Not that I was seeing many exotic destinations myself as a 17 year old. I'd love to have spent the summer holiday hitch-hiking to Pamplona but mainly I was at home, reading more books and revising for my exam. For a brief period time seemed to hang suspended. But then it was autumn once again and the pace quickened. The entrance papers were scheduled for the end of November and I realised that after years of Juddian incarceration, decisions about my future were approaching fast.

I was meant to prepare for the Oxbridge hurdle alongside my A level work. The school made no special allowance for revision in the timetable. Afternoons of free periods, sitting around in the sixth-form common-room, were a complete waste of time. I could work a lot better at home but officially asking for permission seemed doomed to failure. So once or twice I just bunked off. Surely nobody would be bothered to check up on me? Oh yes they would.

There were about half a dozen of us sitting the entrance exams and they took place in a room above the library which was reached by a staircase near to Riddle's study. As I approached the stairs on the Monday morning I saw the headmaster lurking outside his office. He had clearly been waiting for me and he summoned me briskly inside.

Riddle looked grim. There were only ten minutes before my first paper began but it seemed some matter had arisen that was so urgent that he had to discuss it with me at once. For one awful moment I thought he was about to tell me that my mother had died or that my father had been knocked over on the way to work. But no. It was far worse than that. The previous week I had been 'observed absconding from school premises without permission'. It seemed that some spiritual confrère of the creep maths master of three years before had spotted me heading for the station and felt duty bound to inform the headmaster.

As a consequence, declared Riddle, he would have to ask me to return my monitor's tie. I thought he was joking . . . but he never joked. I started to untie the knot. As I did so Riddle opened a drawer and, like some MI5 officer swapping microfilm with the Russians, took out a standard upper-school red, white and blue and ritually exchanged it for my monitor's maroon. Then he showed me out. He didn't bother to wish me good luck or anything like that. As I climbed the stairs I half wondered if the whole exercise had been his idea of a psychological incentive. No, I concluded. The bastard's just a total fucking shit.

I sat my tests that day and the next and then did my best to forget about them. At the end of the week I had a trip down to Brighton for an interview at Sussex, which was a hotbed of subversion as far as Judd was concerned and was accordingly my second choice after University College, Oxford.

It was a bright and frosty morning and strolling around the town in my own clothes on a weekday felt like a foretaste of freedom. The campus at Falmer, all modern, low-level concrete and glass, couldn't remotely have been described as attractive. But in that era it was de rigueur for progressives to be in favour of the brutalist-modernist look in architecture in much the same way as one enthused about the German car industry and Scandinavian attitudes to sex.

My appointment was with Professor Marcus Cunliffe who was the head of English and American studies. So far from being some stern Marxist – like Howard Kirk, the central character in Malcolm Bradbury's hilarious novel *The History Man* – he was a charming listener and courteous questioner who seemed to share all my enthusiasms for American novels and films. We talked for around three-quarters of an hour and he shook my hand warmly when I left. A few days later he sent a letter to the school and Riddle read it to me with as little enthusiasm as possible. It said there would definitely be a place for me there, providing I passed the necessary three A levels. Now at least I had an option whatever Oxford decided.

The following week I went up for my interview at Univ. The trip was presided over by Graham Devlin, a good friend, formerly of Tonbridge school, who was already up reading English but had had to miss a couple of terms after developing hepatitis on a trip to Afghanistan.

We drove first to London for a lunchtime of drinking and hanging out. Then in the late afternoon we headed up Mr Reddy's derided A40, arriving in Oxford after dark. It was foggy and cold. The Michaelmas term had just ended so there weren't that many students around and the university buildings had a rather ghostly and deserted air.

That first night we went out to the house that Devlin had been living in with some friends not far from the Rose Revived pub near Standlake. The evening was great. There was a jukebox in the kitchen and plenty to drink and more dope than I was used to. I fell asleep in an empty bed covered with a spare blanket.

The following morning I looked and felt rough and more joints after breakfast and a few more pints over lunch didn't help. So in the afternoon Devlin took me back into the city to his ex-girlfriend's flat off the Banbury Road. She was a tall and beautiful Scottish girl with long brown hair and brown eyes. She teased me, but took pity on me and found various medications and hangover cures then shoved me in the bath. When I emerged about an hour later bathed, shaved and wearing a clean shirt and a jacket and tie, they decided I was almost presentable.

Graham, who was acting as my personal chauffeur, drove me down to the High Street and dropped me off at Univ. The college quadrangles smelled of damp and overcooked vegetables. My head was beginning to clear but the fog still hadn't lifted and the atmosphere felt Gothic and dark.

All of the interviewees – and 30 years ago the college was still an all-male preserve – had dinner together in hall at one long table. Lights flickered, briefly illuminating rich brown panelling and venerable portraits of past college masters and distinguished fellows. Some of the boys talked loudly, bragging about their schools and who knew whose brother or sister. They all seemed very confident they'd be returning the following year.

My first meeting in the morning was with the principal English tutor Peter Bayley, a charming, erudite man who made notes about undergraduates' essays on the back of fag packets. 'You wrote a long and enthusiastic answer about *Great Expectations*,' he said. 'Would you like to tell me about any other nineteenth-century novels you feel passionate about?' The bowling wasn't quite so innocuous as that opening delivery suggested but talking enthusiastically about *David Copperfield* and *Tess of the D'Urbervilles* for three-quarters of an hour wasn't difficult.

Later there was a general interview with another college fellow who asked me what I read for 'trash'. Brian Mitchell's reply would've been that life was too short to read trash and that you'd have been better off reading *Paradise Lost* but I could tell that would've been too earnest a response for my inquisitor. 'I like Ian Fleming,' I said. 'Especially *Casino Royale* and *Diamonds*

Are Forever.' 'Saratoga,' he said, his eyes lighting up. 'Bond goes to the races.' And the conversation took off.

That evening I met up with Devlin and his ex-girlfriend again in the Banbury Road flat. More of their friends came round, including an attractively mocking and quick-witted woman who made me feel a lot less confident than I was pretending to be on the outside. They were all in their final year and Graham was loaded down with work that he had to catch up on before he came back up in January. There were copies of *Beowulf* and Chambers *Anglo-Saxon Dictionary* and Spenser's *The Faerie Queene*. It all looked very old and gloomy, a bit like the college setting. Is this what I shall have to affect nonchalant familiarity with if I get in? I wondered.

Graham went back to London on the Thursday and I went home alone. On the way I had to change trains at Redhill. Waiting on the platform reminded me of setting off on family holidays to the Isle of Wight with my parents when I was five years old. At the time Redhill, Guildford and indeed anywhere west of Edenbridge had seemed like the edge of the world and beyond. Now adult life with all its intoxicating delights was tantalisingly close at hand.

The next day my father brought an early-morning cup of tea into my room as he always did on schooldays. My alarm clock had just gone off and Radio One was playing in the background. Rod Stewart. T. Rex. Tony Blackburn. A letter had come for me and I think we both knew what it was. My father put it down on the bedside table and left me alone.

Head still half under the blankets, I picked up the envelope and opened it. It was from John Albery, the University College tutor for admissions. He said he was writing to confirm that the college was 'delighted' to offer me a place to read English the following October. I had to pass O level French, otherwise the only remaining requirement was that I should get two A levels. At Grade E.

I put the letter down and lay there in the dark for a few moments. Up until that point I hadn't really known if I wanted to go to Oxford even if I had been accepted. Now I knew I wouldn't be able to turn it down. Leigh Primary School seemed an awfully long way away. Two A levels. At Grade E. It would be a stroll. The game was effectively over. Riddle. Taylor. Sackett. Reddy. They'd lost. And I'd won. By an innings.

The final two terms at Judd were the only enjoyable phase of my entire seven years at grammar school. I drifted through the days like a man whose bags were packed and already in the departure lounge. While friends had to sweat and worry over their upcoming exams, my big challenge was already over and my future settled. I had to pass French O level but with a little bit of extra tutoring that suddenly seemed easy and straightforward.

My parents sold their house in Leigh and moved to Tunbridge Wells. And I got an evening and weekend job as a porter at the Kent and Sussex Hospital in Pembury. It was hard work with 7.30 a.m starts, lighting the big ovens in the Victorian ward kitchens. The smell of gas and porridge and disinfectant – smells that reminded me of my grandmother's last weeks in hospital five years before – was hard to stomach after four hours' sleep and a good night out on a Friday or Saturday. But the job meant that I had cash in my pocket on both weekends and schooldays. I had new clothes to wear, cigarettes to share, LPs to lend and each day I could luxuriate lazily in my situation. There were still a few pointless skirmishes with the authorities but I could feel their power over me waning by the week.

One February afternoon there was a formal ceremony to mark the opening of a new sixth-form block and F.H. Taylor was wheeled out of retirement as guest of honour. I did my best to avoid him but he sought me out anyway and insisted on shaking me by the hand. 'I gather you're off to some suburb of Bletchley,' he chortled as if we'd always been the best of chums. I'd love to have come out with a brilliantly witty riposte but Riddle was close by and then the moment was gone. It was tempting to regard Taylor as a kindly old buffer who'd always had our best interests at heart but I've no doubt that if he'd had his way I'd have been kicked out before my O levels.

My hospital earnings gave me the opportunity to have a bet each weekend and on many weekdays too. On 2,000 Guineas day in May 1972 I was polishing the floors of the geriatric wards in Pembury but I found time to switch on a TV and watch Willie Carson ride High Top to victory by half a length. In second place was my selection Roberto, who was trained by Vincent O'Brien and ridden by the Australian jockey Bill Williamson.

As every racing historian will know, Williamson, or Weary Willie as the bookies called him, was meant to ride Roberto again in the Derby on 7 June. He was injured in May but then recovered and had supposedly been promised his Derby mount was safe by Roberto's owner John Galbreath, the proprietor of the Pittsburgh Pirates baseball team. But then, at the 11th hour, the wily Lester Piggott managed to jock him off.

Racing writers in general and the *Telegraph* correspondent in particular were outraged but I was with Lester. Not only was he the better jockey, the ultimate Epsom specialist who'd already won the Derby five times, two of them for O'Brien, but once again he'd done the indecent thing and trumped the nice guy's ace. It was the sort of behaviour that Riddle and Taylor would have heartily disapproved of, so naturally I warmed to it. And plunged on Roberto with a large chunk of my hospital wages, money I was saving to travel with later that summer.

Lester won, of course, though only by a matter of inches and only after a titanic battle with the subsequent Prix de l'Arc De Triomphe winner, Rheingold. It was one of the most dramatic and violent finishes in Derby history but all that mattered to me was that Lester Piggott and Vincent O'Brien, the incomparable duo who'd given us Sir Ivor and Nijinsky, were supreme at Epsom once again.

By Derby Day our A levels had started. The questions seemed dull and formulaic compared with the Oxford entrance paper. We had three or four weeks off school while the exams took place, then we had to go back for five final pointless days at the beginning of July. On the last Friday assorted services and valedictory presentations had been arranged and all sixth formers were expected to attend. But I never got that far. It was a fine summer morning – too good to waste much of it stewing in the hall listening to E.P. Riddle. So shortly after break, a friend and I just walked out through the front gates, ostentatiously taking off our ties as we went and throwing them in a dustbin.

We passed Riddle's office and the parked cars of various members of staff. A friendly but ineffectual R.E. teacher was scurrying past in the opposite direction. He looked at us nervously as if he ought to object but then decided not to. 'Goodbye, Sir,' we said pleasantly. 'Have a good life.' No thunderbolts cracked in the sky. No super-posse of headmasters, complete with gowns, canes and mortarboards, saddled up and set off in pursuit. We were free at last.

We drove into Tunbridge Wells and went down to the alley behind the Pantiles to what was then still a richly atmospheric old pub called the Sussex Arms. Black marketeers and American servicemen used to frequent it during the war when it was nicknamed the Sussex Shades and was the place to buy condoms, gum and chocolate bars. It's long since been renovated and ruined by a brewery but in 1972 it still had a relaxed and louche atmosphere that we loved.

The landlord, a large, slow, bearded man with a big dog, had just opened up. He was a racing enthusiast and as usual he had a copy of the *Sporting Life* open on the bar. We bought a pint and lit a cigarette and took the paper outside and sat on the steps in the warm sunshine and it had never felt so good to be alive.

Other friends joined us at the pub and then we all went out to lunch. Later on that afternoon I walked back up the hill through the town past Goulden and Curry, Stationers and Books, past The Hole In The Wall pub and the former lads and ageing hippies in Coffee Corner. I walked past Weekes department store and the central station and the Court School of Ballroom Dancing. And I walked up Mount Pleasant past Nelson Wingate opticians, past D'Ambrosio's coffee bar and the Essoldo cinema. And I walked on past the Opera House and the windows of

Chiesmans, where, in the carpet department in the afternoon heat, my father, jacket off, would be lugging rolls of Axminster broadloom. The shop, as usual, too mean to equip him and his assistant with a few porters to do the heavy lifting.

Alex was 57 years old and, in Philip Larkin's immortal words, he was 'weighed down with obligations and necessary observances' and truly a man 'whose first coronary' was 'coming like Christmas'. But he had given me the gift of life and, thanks to him and my mother and their encouragement, patience and support, I'd reached the gate that led out into the world beyond a small town. Now all I had to do was turn the key.

CHAPTER FOURTEEN

It had been decided that we would travel up from Euston on the 8:20 breakfast train. Or the 'knife and fork' as Mel called it. Melvin Kenneth Smith. Actor. Comedian. Director. Film-maker. Entrepreneur. Connoisseur of late nights, large brandies, fat cigars and all things London and metropolitan. A keen gambler. A dedicated punter and life-long student of the Turf, which is hardly surprising given that his father was the proprietor of a small chain of betting shops in west London.

In the early '70s Mel had spent several years theoretically studying experimental psychology at New College, Oxford. Here his brain had been one of the sharpest even if his attendance at tutorials had been sporadic and frequently curtailed by more pressing engagements at Sandown, Kempton and Ascot Heath.

I first got to know Mel in the winter of 1973, halfway through my first year at university. We had a racing passion to unite us along with a love of the stage and he soon became an emphatic and emphatically generous friend. Ten years later I was on the verge of getting married and I suppose it was inevitable that horse racing should play some part in the rites of passage and inevitable, too, that Mel should have a primary role in directing the pre-nuptial events. His wedding present to me? An attempted betting coup at Haydock Park racecourse in Lancashire. To be embarked on by a team of four. On a dark winter Thursday, a December jump-racing day, 48 hours before I was expected to be waiting at the church. Who could possibly have asked for more?

There has always been a heightened and Gatsbyesque quality to Mel. A man not given to small or half-hearted gestures. At Oxford some people mentioned his name in awed tones while others, the snooty and the irredeemably twee, seemed to regard him with a mixture of disdain and alarm. To an Oxbridge environment not short of strangulated vowels and sub-Brideshead self-consciousness he brought an exhilarating energy and directness allied to a wicked sense of humour.

Mel may have been passionate about betting and racing but he was also passionate about the theatre. He was a brilliant student director and to watch his productions, or better still to participate in them, was to be left in no doubt that of all our contemporaries, be their ambitions clearly defined or scarcely half-formed, Mel was bound for fame. He was equally at ease with Shakespeare and Jean Genet, with Tom Stoppard and a Broadway musical. And where many students were happy to make their mark with camp costume dramas in college gardens or earnestly experimental efforts in some draughty loft over a garage, M.K. Smith was already dreaming of the West End.

Mel's aura at Oxford was helped by his appearance, which included shoulder-length hair – this was 1973 after all – and his habit of going around in a suit which was as excitingly different to all that crushed velvet and brushed denim as the lads' stay-pressed suits and Ben Sherman shirts had been at dances in Tonbridge in 1968. Mel's ensemble would typically include an open-necked shirt with a massive '70s collar, flared trousers and platform-heeled shoes. A look much favoured by his circle and one that I soon grew fond of myself.

An unexpected bonus of Mel's company was that I also quickly got to know his closest Oxford friend, David Tupman, who was studying politics, philosophy and economics at New College.

Another man with a very sharp mind – Dave, like myself, was an absolute racing fanatic with a splendid undergraduate penchant for gambling and leisure. He grew up partly in Sevenoaks, not more than six miles away from Leigh and Tonbridge, and he too started betting as a teenager and incurred the disapproving wrath of first school masters and then, bank managers. An unfailingly good-humoured student, with a rakish James Hunt air, David remains the most loyal and dependable friend I've ever known and his behaviour doesn't change whether he's up or down, in life or on the track.

In February 1973 Mel, David and one or two others came to see a play I'd put on – an absurdist, experimental effort in a draughty loft over a garage. We went out to dinner afterwards to an Italian restaurant where Mel seemed to enjoy an impressively familial relationship with the owner, who could himself always be relied upon to present an impressively large bill.

We talked about a race coming up at Wincanton on the Thursday of that week. A Champion Hurdle trial likely to feature the reigning title-holder Bula, who was trained by Fred Winter and had won the championship for each of the last two seasons. Mel mentioned airily that he was planning to go down to Wincanton to place a bet on Bula with the on-course bookies. He said he was hoping to get on two or three hundred. I was stunned and impressed, not just by the sum involved but by the seeming indifference to tutorials, lectures and the minutiae of college life, not to mention his willingness to drive all the way to Somerset and back for an afternoon's racing. (Bula only scrambled home as it happened, at odds-on too, which must have resulted in a tense and sweaty three minutes for Mel, and Winter scotched plans to run him in the Champion Hurdle that year.)

Just over a week later Mel and Dave were planning to go racing at Newbury on a Friday afternoon and I was invited to go with them. It was a simple decision really. Either say yes and start living right there or be a timid first-year student and say no. I said yes. I had a tutorial at nine o' clock that Friday morning so I stayed up most of the previous night to write my essay. Then, when the academic encounter was over, I grabbed breakfast and a bath, ironed a clean shirt and pulled on my only suit, the one I had to wear for exams, matriculation ceremonies and so on. Pausing only to buy a *Sporting Life*, I dashed round to the house in St John's Street, not far from where Graham Greene once lived, which was where we were to set out from.

Mel, to his fury, had been grounded by a college summons but was determined to go dog racing at Oxford Stadium that evening. So David and I went without him, Dave resplendent in a grey suit and white open-necked shirt. This was to be no Tattersalls or Silver Ring outing. We went into the Members' Enclosure and I remember wondering exactly how I was going to pay for it all. David backed the first two winners, Ballyhoura Hill and Keep Time, and then lost what he'd won on the next few races. I think I had just the one winner and to relatively modest stakes, but there was enough cash to keep the vodka and gin flowing throughout the afternoon and I loved every minute of it.

A few weeks later, with Mel at the helm this time, we went to Cheltenham on Gold Cup day. It was my first-ever visit to the course. A once seen never to be forgotten sight. A day of fine weather and clear skies, of crowds and booze and noise and betting and intensity and racing the like of which I'd never experienced in the flesh before. The Dikler, saddled by Fulke Walwyn himself, trainer of the great Mill House, scored a thrilling Gold Cup victory, storming up the hill to beat Fred Winter's King George VI Chase champion Pendil in the dying strides. It was Walwyn's fifth and final Gold Cup success and no less a horse than L'Escargot, dual winner in 1970 and '71, was among the beaten runners.

Back in 1973 few jump jockeys were interested in being advised to cut down on their post-race carousing and enthusiastic racegoers did their best to keep up with them. The old wooden bars in the Cheltenham stand were a kind of Grade One-listed fire risk. They were spectacularly inadequate when it came to coping with the huge crush of thirsty punters but those same over-crowded rooms, with their basket chairs, their selections of canapés and *bouchées de la reine* and their array of oysters, lobster and bottles of splash, were brimful of atmosphere and life.

With Mel the drink was always champagne and not just any old label either. It had to be Bollinger or not at all. More bottles were consumed at Kempton, Sandown Park and White City dogs during the Easter vacation and we drank it to toast Mel's success with a big treble on Owen Dudley, winner of Newmarket's Wood Ditton Stakes for Noel Murless, a horse called Golden Master, trained by old Bill Marshall, and a staying hurdler called Parthenon, who won a three-mile handicap at Cheltenham's April meeting. Mel bought a car with the proceeds.

That summer we visited Lingfield, Ascot and the July course at Newmarket and the following March we were at the Festival on Gold Cup day once again, enjoying a thumping win on Sir Peter O'Sullevan's little Epsom-trained four-year-old Attivo, who made nearly all the running in the Triumph Hurdle. Called home memorably on the BBC by his unflappably professional owner and one of the most popular of all Cheltenham successes.

In the big race Mel plunged on The Dikler to repeat his triumph of the year before, but this time the massive chestnut, who had something of a Mill House stamp about him, found himself in front too soon when his great rival Pendil was brought down three out. He was picked off approaching the last by the New Zealand-bred Captain Christy, who was trained in Ireland by Pat Taaffe (who'd retired from race riding in 1970) and ridden by his fellow Irishman Bobby Beasley, who'd won the 1961 Grand National on Nicolaus Silver. More names from my racing and TV-watching childhood now writ large in front of my eyes.

Captain Christy made a terrible mistake at the final jump, which seemed to have swung the race in Mel's and The Dikler's favour. But then he quickened again on the run-in, showing a change of pace that Arkle himself would've been proud of, and beat Fulke Walwyn's runner going away. It was an unforgettable day for Beasley, a jockey who had battled regularly with alcoholism, eventually winning the fight, and an ecstatic outcome for the Irish who were celebrating their fourth Gold Cup win in five years. The drink flowed and flowed. And not just in Cheltenham either but throughout the surrounding countryside. 'Have you seen the Rover? I seem to have mislaid it,' enquired one glowing punter with a Cork accent as he wandered out of a pub near Burford and disappeared into a field around 11.30 that night.

Mel had greeted his defeat with the defiant good humour that he brought to every reversal, insisting that at such moments it was more important than ever to consume as much alcohol as possible and outface disaster with style. By the time the 1975 Cheltenham Festival came around he'd left Oxford and set off on the high road to London but David and I made a dedicated trip to Prestbury Park, where, like 40,000 other racegoers, we were drenched by torrential rain, mud washing up over our shoes and trouser legs.

In the SunAlliance Hurdle, rescheduled from the abandoned opening day, Mick O'Toole pulled off a mighty gamble with a horse called Davy Lad, who hadn't run for five months. In the Gold Cup itself Jim Dreaper's Ten Up galloped through the puddles to beat Fred Winter's pair, Bula and Soothsayer, and then after that the stewards called it off. But not before I'd seen the Duchess of Westminster, looking identical to the TV images of Arkle's triumphs, collect the Gold Cup from a luminary of Piper Heidseck champagne. The ceremony was presided over by the priceless figure of Major General Sir Randle Fielden, who was Cheltenham's and jump racing's senior panjandrum at the time. Rainwater dripping down over his bowler hat, he held his microphone at arm's length as if it might be a dangerous weapon and delivered his speech with all the animation of a water buffalo with lockjaw.

I've been to all three days of every Festival since 1975 with the exception of 1977, when I was in America, and the 1978 Gold Cup, which had to be cancelled due to bad weather and took place in April instead. I don't think David has missed a single

Festival meeting since 1978, when he was on his honeymoon in Paris. That year he drove back to Gloucestershire on the Wednesday night, enjoying the bemused support of his wife, only to wake up on the Thursday morning to find the Cotswolds blanketed in snow.

Mel hasn't been to every Cheltenham. Work has often intervened and there was a period in the late '80s and early '90s when he temporarily withdrew from the scene. But for a seven- or eight-year span following our university lives we went racing regularly, taking in everywhere from Salisbury to Goodwood and from Windsor evening meetings to Catterick Bridge. Sometimes it was profitable. Sometimes it was disastrous. But it was always fun.

As Mel started to become famous thanks to his burgeoning TV appearances on *Not The Nine O'Clock News*, his trips to the races took on a slightly different complexion. Some racegoers clearly felt his media exposure made him public property entitling any idiot in the bar to bang him over the head with a rolled-up newspaper and chortle, 'Got any news then? Yo ho ho.'

Then there were those slyly self-promoting individuals, who would like you to think they're racing insiders, who started sidling up to him as if they'd known each other for years and passing on tips in a suitably confidential tone. Mel, who'd always been a good judge and more than capable of arriving at his own views about a race, had less time to study the form than might've been the case when he was a student. But as soon as he stepped on to a racecourse he could rely on being surrounded by friends, all with their sundry advices about 'Cecil's best two year old' or 'Winter's best novice' or some maiden three year old that a top jockey had been touting to his punters. Needless to say, not all of these good things were any more reliable than the good friends recommending them.

By 1982 Mel had shares in one or two horses of his own and one deranged winter's day we travelled all the way up to Catterick in North Yorkshire to watch one of these animals given a nice 'easy' in a novice hurdle in preparation for a possible gamble next time out. The trainer and jockey had rock-solid credentials within the northern racing community and later that day Mel was approached by another trainer, one of the foremost of the era, who offered to find a horse for him, price range to be agreed, and to train it for nothing for the first year at least. The implication was that gambles could be landed right up to the highest level providing the raw material was good enough.

This self-same brilliant if eccentric trainer had a runner in the last, a two-mile Bumper, and his representative was expected to start favourite. We would almost certainly have backed it too had the trainer not helpfully warned us that the contest was 'expected' to go to another in the field who just happened to be trained by his brother-in-law. It worked out exactly as predicted. Our new confidant's runner went off as the market leader and finished second or third if I recall. And the brother-in-law's horse won at something like 8–1 or bigger.

Scandalous? That depends on your point of view. Anyone who imagines that every horse race has always been decided strictly on its merits is, I'm afraid, dangerously and intolerably naive. Of course an element of chicanery clings to the Turf. That's one of its main selling points. And callow researchers for television documentaries, brandishing their two months' acquaintance with the sport and claiming to have uncovered the shocking corruption at its heart, should be met with derision rather than trepidation and alarm.

It's rightly said that the betting public need to have faith in the fundamental basis of the game if they're to continue to invest. But it's still gambling and there's no law that says the favourites and odds-on chances will always win. Punters have to be responsible for their actions. Most of them are not that bothered by the occasional act of spivvery anyway. It doesn't go on all the time and certainly not in the biggest and most valuable races where everything's trying. But a little bit of devilment round the edges adds colouring and flavour to the mix. Take away all the chancers and conmen – who are as likely to come from Mayfair as Moss Side – and racing would eventually become as faultlessly bland as the Badminton three-day event.

And so it was that come December 1983 Mel felt that a wedding could not really be entered into without a major racing experience taking place first. Any full day at the track would've been special but the prospect of a touch being involved added intrigue to the fun. We'd had a few shots at it before with one of Mel's own horses, the hero of the Catterick work-out who was meant to be 'off' next time out in a novice hurdle at Kelso. We all backed him but he was turned over in a photo finish. 'Object. Object,' urged a confederate as he came puffing up the steps to meet Mel at the top of the Kelso stand. It was a desperate ploy and an unsuccessful one, but the pay-off was not long coming.

A few weeks later the horse lined up in another novice hurdle race at Perth. It was only a moderate affair but it's not an afternoon I shall forget lightly. That January I had broken my back falling down some stairs in London and then slipping over on an icy pavement, all in the space of the same day. The fractured vertebrae didn't heal as quickly as they should've done and in April I found myself tilted painfully out of shape and back in St Stephen's Hospital on London's Fulham Road.

Twenty years ago there was still a rather repressive element to the treatment of spinal injuries and I spent the first four or five days lying flat on my back pumped up with painkillers. It was supposed to be restful but it was also tedious and gave you the feeling your whole body was seizing up. The Perth hurdle race coincided with my confinement and a combination of boredom allied to the pleasurable cocktail of drugs – laced with visitors' alcohol – encouraged me to plunge more recklessly on Mel's horse than I might otherwise have done. Communicating with him on an old-fashioned portable ward phone that was wheeled over to my bed, I asked for £200 to win on his runner along with £80 on a stable companion who was running in the first and an £80 double on the two of them.

To find out how I'd done I had to tune into the racing results on the hospital radio. Perth was the last meeting to come up and Mel's horse was in the final race on the card. The stable companion's result came first and he'd won at 9–2. The announcer then worked his way through the details of four more low-grade contests until finally reaching the concluding race of the day. And yes, sweet to report, the touch had been landed albeit at the cramped odds of 2–1.

High on excitement and dihydrocodeine I decided I wanted to tell somebody about my winnings which came to well over a thousand pounds. Summoning the portable phone would've meant everyone overhearing the conversation. But then I remembered there was a pay-phone in the corridor at the end of the ward. So, intent on ringing Mel or Dave or both, I got off the bed – unaided – and started walking up the room – unaided. These were the first steps I'd taken for a week and the nurses, seeing my stiff, steady but unannounced progress, came rushing over to check I was all right. 'You're walking,' they exclaimed with much cooing and admiration. 'How wonderful! You're back on your feet again. You're getting better.' I assured them that it was all down to the power of prayer.

I wish I could say that all subsequent racing scenarios culminated with similar miracle-working thousand-pound winners but, predictably, that hasn't been the case. I say 'predictably' because as any experienced punter will know racehorses cannot read the script in advance and the vast majority of coups and touches are never even reported because most of them end in failure. This is probably why the news that some horse might be the business at Haydock, and that we might be able to cash in on this intelligence just before the chiming of bells, didn't exactly thrill my wife-to-be Emma. Nor did it convince David's wife Clare and other friends and associates who had seen where racing generally led us, and didn't share our romantic attachment to the Turf. There was also a subtext to their unease. A concern as to what state we would be in, and in particular what shape I'd be in, after a day's racing and drinking in Lancashire only 48 hours before the wedding.

At the start of the week we tried to play things down with assurances that in all probability the Haydock trip wouldn't even happen. Mel joked about the traditional concept of a stag night with its requirement that 'we should all be sick and lose our trousers'.

When it came to it on the night of Wednesday, 14 December we had a remarkably restrained and civilised evening. We went out to dinner and to a cabaret, drank a bit and then went back to Mel's house in Waldemar Avenue in Fulham, where we drank a bit more and swapped nostalgic anecdotes. But underneath our surface good manners there was a powerful desire to go for it. An urging fuelled to irresistible proportions by telephone conversations with an informed friend and a consideration of the Haydock card in the *Evening Standard*.

At some point that night Emma gave the jaunt her blessing. And at 7.30 the following morning, after little more than four and a half hours' sleep, I jumped into a cab on the King's Road and set off for Euston. It was a cold, grey and thoroughly wintry day and the rush-hour traffic was bad. I very nearly didn't get to the station in time.

Running across the concourse at 8.15 and looking around wildly for the others, I suddenly heard a stentorian voice yelling my name. And waiting up ahead by the ticket barrier I saw the burly Sid – I have to call him Sid – who was the real architect of the comedy to come. David, who was to be my best man, was with him. Like the fabulously generous personality he is, Dave was carrying a magnum of champagne. A first-class return ticket had been purchased on my behalf and with less than a minute to spare the three of us tore up the platform and piled into the restaurant car of the Glasgow train, where Mel, *Sporting Life* to hand, eyes twinkling and already alive to the incipient lunacy of the venture, was seated at a table for four. We were on our way.

CHAPTER FIFTEEN

Sid, who sat by Mel's side, was in a very serious mood. Indeed his expression was so military and Freddie Forsyth that we wouldn't have been surprised to find he had an AK Walther Automatic hidden inside his trenchcoat pocket.

Sid – it wasn't his real name – had been a brilliant classics scholar at Oxford but he left after a year to pursue a career as a professional punter and bookie. He was the man supposedly in the know, with contacts among the faces, indeed a face himself. It was he who had gleaned information about the intended job at Haydock Park, and had proposed ourselves as the ideal men, having no known contact with the owner and trainer, to put the connections money on at the track. Here, we would also be allowed to have a bit on for ourselves. As and when Sid instructed us, that is.

An obliging steward poured Dave's bottle and as rain fell on the country outside, we tucked into every last cholesterol-rich mouthful of the full British Rail breakfast. At this point all David and I, and possibly Mel too, knew for certain was that we were going to Haydock Park. Such was Sid's mania for secrecy that we didn't know the name of our horse or the race it was running in. That would come later. What he did inform us was that we would be getting out not at Warrington Bank Quay, the normal station for anyone travelling to Haydock, but at Crewe some 30 miles south. It appeared that Sid was worried that the bookies might have spies on the platform at Warrington or perhaps hiding in the Travellers Fare lounge. Should they spot us disembarking together and then see us in cahoots at the races they'd conclude we were the 'smart boys' up from London. And then the odds we'd be offered would contract and our plot would begin to unravel.

So Crewe it was. Here, we were to meet up with Sid's main cohort in the scam, a gentleman called Roy who was apparently a wily punter around the Midlands and North West and who would be driving us on to Haydock. I imagine we all had an idea of what Roy might be like. Not quite Steve McQueen in *The Cincinatti Kid* maybe but still something sharp and Runyonesque. A J.J. or a Kid Twist. Instead we were confronted by a grey-haired and conservative-looking gentleman in his late 50s who had thick, black-framed glasses and a pronounced Black Country accent. He was wearing a long, black, funereal overcoat and his car, appropriately enough, was a black Rover. We all climbed in – Sid in the front; Mel, David and myself in the back – and then Roy conveyed us at a steady pace up the M6.

David and I had to be careful not to catch Mel's eye in case we all started giggling. Mel and Sid were both on the well-built side and as we rumbled up the motorway in Roy's Rover, doing at least 40 miles an hour, we must have looked more like a group of old-fashioned communist party officials on their way to an iron and steel conference in Bratislava than a team of ice-cool punters on their way to collect.

Cheshire's rain-sodden fields and leafless trees gradually gave way to industrial Lancashire and at exit 23 we turned off the motorway and pulled in through the gates to the adjacent Haydock racetrack. Roy parked his car and then headed off to gather intelligence. The rest of us headed for the bar.

Haydock is a proper racecourse. It may be flat. The view beyond the far side, mainly of speeding motorway traffic and the Post House hotel, may not be picturesque but the crowds are always good, including plenty of knowledgeable Mancunian and Merseyside racing enthusiasts. The track's fair though the fences take some jumping and the quality of the sponsored steeplechases, even when there aren't that many runners, is always high. Inside the Members' stand in 1983 there were coal fires in winter, willing and capable bar staff and officials and a lip-smacking aura of speculation and brass.

We filled up with Bollinger and plates of poached salmon and studied the card. I seem to remember we all backed the winner in the first and Mel may have backed the second winner too. The third race was intriguing. A two-and-a-half-mile handicap hurdle with more than 20 runners. There were a few predictable favourites from the bigger stables but, as David and I hesitated in front of the bookies, we suddenly remembered that Roy had given us a tip for this one. Something called Bold Illusion representing a small Shropshire yard, amateur-ridden and predicted to go off at 50–1, according to the *Sporting Life*. Yet on the boards in front of our eyes he was trading at 25–1 and 20–1. Then one or two firms cut him to 16s. We hastily looked up his form. Unluckily brought down last time out when holding a prominent position in a two-and-a-half-mile hurdle race at Bangor. His first sign of ability since winning over two miles and six furlongs at Kelso the previous November. On soft ground. Today's going was very soft.

I think David stuck on at least £50 or maybe £100 on the nose. I had something like £20 each way. And he won comfortably. Taking it up approaching the last and going a couple of lengths clear on the run-in. Well, well, we thought. Good old Roy. We owe'd him an apology. As well as a drink. Thanks to him at least we two would be going home that night with some Christmas expenses in our pockets.

There was no time to celebrate Bold Illusion's victory though. Not just yet. The fourth race was a staying chase but the fifth was our race. The big one. The coup. And while the fourth was being run we had orders to attend upon Maestro Sid. In a cubicle in the downstairs gents' cloakroom.

Our man was already ensconced when we arrived and we had to knock on the door to be admitted. Waiting until there were no other punters around to see us, lest they should imagine we were either desperate for a line of Bolivian marching powder or about to engage in some act of strenuous sexual congress – neither option as uncommon in racecourse lavatories as some unworldly racing types might think. A few moments later Mel arrived and then, as they say, the plot thickened.

The fifth race was a selling hurdle, the lowest kind of contest in the programme book and the type of event normally contested by the slowest and least talented horses in training. The prize money for a seller is minimal but all the runners have a reserve put on them and the winner is offered for sale straight after the race. If he fails to make his reserve, his owners keep him. If the bidding goes higher than the reserve but the owners want to keep him anyway they have to pay to get him back. The real business of a seller though is in the betting ring. It's the kind of race that gives a small stable a chance to land a blow with a moderate horse, especially if they can get a price about their runner that underestimates its actual ability.

The Haydock seller that day was over two and three-quarter miles, which would feel more like three on heavy ground in December. And our horse, our great hope, was a five-year-old gelding called Trinculo. No Arkle or Mill House or Nijinsky. In fact an almost entirely unheralded and unremembered name in racing history. Except to us.

Trinculo, who was a half-brother to a St Leger runner-up, had been sold out of a Newmarket flat-racing yard and was now with the stable of a Gloucestershire-based trainer who had some form in events of this kind. And who would've said, perfectly reasonably, that he was just trying to do his best for Trinculo and his owners. And thanks to Sid and Roy it was Mel, David and myself who were going to represent those owners' interests in the betting ring.

Sid reached into his trenchcoat pockets and produced three blocks of money wrapped up in old pages of the *Sporting Life*. He gave one to me, one to David and one to Mel, explaining that they each contained several thousand pounds' worth of readies. So far that afternoon I'd been betting in maximums of ten and twenty. Wouldn't the bookies be a little suspicious when I suddenly transformed into a high-roller and attempted to unload such a sizeable wedge? I could see that David had similar reservations but Sid was in no state to entertain doubts of any kind.

The one stipulation of the coup was that our cash, or to be more precise the owners' cash, couldn't be wagered on course until the first show of odds came through from the betting shops. This was because the trainer's money was being placed in a string of smaller bets away from the track. He wanted to get the biggest price available and if the on-course gamble was already underway, the odds offered to his punters would be appreciably shorter.

When we went upstairs into the ring we were told to spread out into a line and allocated four or five bookmaking pitches each. Sid would be furthest away over by the racecourse betting shop, which would receive the first set of prices on the race, including Trinculo's odds, from the off-course offices. At that moment Sid would give us the signal to go in. 'When I move you move,' he explained to Mel theatrically. 'When Mel moves, David moves and when David moves, Jamie moves . . . '

'And then do I move again?' asked Mel mischievously.

'No,' thundered Sid. 'You move when I move . . . '

'And then Jamie moves?'

'And then David moves,' corrected Sid.

'And then we all move together?' suggested Mel, but Sid wasn't laughing.

We spread out as ordered, our jacket pockets bulging with dough. Whenever I caught Mel's eye he started scratching the side of his nose like Paul Newman surreptitiously acknowledging his sidekicks in *The Sting*. By this point he was practically weeping with laughter but David and I were desperately trying to keep a straight face especially as Sid kept turning round and glaring at us severely.

Betting was non-existent until about ten or twelve minutes

before the race when the on-course bookies started chalking up their odds. Sid had assured us that Trinculo would open up at anything up to 14–1. Instead the best price available on the boards was a niggardly 9–2 and some firms were quoting 4–1. Either the trainer's wagers had been much bigger than expected or something had gone seriously awry. Trinculo's chance was meant to be negligible, a secret to all but the innermost circle of conspirators. So had somebody grassed things up to the bookies? And should we even continue with the gamble given that none of us were going to get anything like the value Sid and Roy had bargained for?

A red-faced Sid came bustling back down the line for an earnest consultation with Mel. Then the word was passed on. The bets were to go ahead. Very well then. Taking a deep breath, I advanced towards the pitch of Mr Francis Habbershawe, an excellent northern bookmaker with whom I'd had £20 on Bold Illusion earlier. Hoping my voice wouldn't crack, I thrust about a quarter of Sid's stake up towards him and asked for the 9–2 about Trinculo. So far from being perturbed or suspicious, Habbershawe accepted the money and dropped it in his satchel in one fluent and unbroken gesture. It was the same with the other pitches where I swiftly rid myself of the rest of the cash and I believe Mel and David found the odds-makers similarly co-operative in their quest to get on.

This was a worrying sign. An attempted touch by the men in the know, the smart money, the faces up from London, ought to spread panic around the ring with the bookies frantically rubbing out prices and attempting to lay off with one another. Yet the Trinculo gamble seemed to inspire no such alarm. We even saw one pitch actually push the price out after we'd backed it.

One of the reasons for the fiasco, it later transpired, was that there was another fancied horse in the race. A horse trained by a certain M.C. or Martin Pipe and ridden by one Peter Scudamore. At the time we were only just beginning to come to terms with Pipe's prodigious hunger for winners. In 1981 he'd landed a touch in the Triumph Hurdle at the Cheltenham

Festival, winning it with a 66–1 outsider called Baron Blakeney. By the winter of 1983 the West Country bookmaker's son had begun his assault on the numerical charts and it seemed that no selling or juvenile hurdle was too moderate for him to run a horse in and no pot – be it north, south, east or west – too humble for his yard to aim at. At Haydock he did for us spectacularly.

We all gathered to watch the race on the terracing outside the Members' bar. The trainer and his son joined us there, introducing themselves with smiles and handshakes and they both seemed very pleasant. The two-and-three-quarter-mile start was on the far side of the track. The race wasn't off until three o'clock and by then it was an increasingly dark and gloomy December afternoon. Entirely appropriate weather really in which to watch our money go west. Well, not much of ours personally in the case of David and myself, but plenty for Sid and Roy and their contacts and for Mel too, who'd loyally committed his own funds to the cause.

Trinculo never looked remotely like winning. When they came past the winning post the first time around he was already struggling and nearer last place than first. 'Don't worry,' said the trainer's son, turning round to us and smiling encouragingly. 'He always runs like this on the first circuit.' What he didn't add was that he'd be running pretty much the same way on the second circuit too. To be fair to the horse and his trainer he did manage a brief push towards the leaders down the back stretch and at one point had closed up into fourth. But then the Pipe runner took charge, drawing several lengths clear around the bend and into the home straight and then going further and further away. I think he won by at least 12 lengths. Well backed too from something like 7–2 to 9–4 favourite. Trinculo was unplaced.

The trainer hurried off sheepishly to greet his loser. Up on the terracing conversation was difficult. Sid, conscious of Mel's losses not to mention the blow to his reputation and judgement, was sawing the air with his hands and offering this explanation and that. 'Don't worry about it, Sid,' said Mel mercilessly. 'Five thousand pounds is a cheap price to pay for an afternoon in your company.'

Let it not be said though that M.K. Smith is a sour or unsporting loser. His manifesto that day, as it has been on every other good, sublime or ruinous racing occasion, was to head for the bar and bash on regardless. This we did. Bottle following bottle. Sid still explaining. An apologetic trainer joining us for a glass but unable, as I recall, to illuminate Trinculo's defeat. The losing jockey joining us for a while too. Looking, we couldn't help feeling, inappropriately cheerful and on good terms with himself. Looking, come to think of it, like a man who'd backed the winner of the selling hurdle and to good money too.

Sid tried to justify himself by promising there would be other better organised and more remunerative coups in future. Mel kept teasing him. Sid got more prickly. And we all kept drinking.

As the afternoon drew in, Roy reappeared. The excellent and much-maligned Roy who'd at least been right about Bold Illusion and who'd remained sober throughout the day. This was just as well as he had to drive us back down the M6 to Crewe for our journey home. We arrived at the station to find we had an hour to wait for the next service to Euston. And, bidding farewell to Roy, ended up in the Florida-themed cocktail bar of the hotel across the road. Here, we knocked back drinks with parasols in, while outside seasonal snowflakes began falling on Cheshire.

When we did take our seats on the train, a steward rushed up excitedly with four menus and invited us to place our orders for dinner. Thank you very much, we said, but we wouldn't be needing dinner. We'd be eating in London later. But this is a full dining-car service, gushed the steward. Well, that's great, we said again, but we really didn't need dinner just yet. The steward looked disconsolate. This is a full dining-car service, he repeated. And the chief steward would have to be sent for. He disappeared up the carriage.

As the train gathered speed, the four of us sat there and kept on chatting. From where I was sitting I could see up the aisle in the direction from which the chief steward would be coming.

Mel, who had his back to him, leaned across and touched my hand. 'Just tell me when you see he's on his way,' he said. 'He's on his way now,' I said, spotting an important-looking official striding down the aisle.

Without interrupting our conversation, Mel took a £20 note out of his pocket and waved it in the air.

'I'm sorry, sir, but unless you're eating you'll really have to move . . . ' began the chief steward. Then he saw the £20. 'Right,' he said, crisply pocketing the cash. 'Perhaps you gentlemen would like a little snack with your drinks?'

'Perhaps we would,' agreed Mel graciously.

'I'll see what I can arrange,' said the chief steward. And little more than ten minutes later he reappeared with a silver salver bearing a display of immaculately cut and appetising-looking steak sandwiches, which we were only too happy to polish off. Away-daying executives being force-fed the usual British Rail 'fried fillet of plaice with lemon wedge and chipped potatoes' looked on, green with envy.

We needed a temporary break from champagne so after the sandwiches Mel and I headed for the buffet. 'Have you got any vodka on this train?' asked Mel.

'Of course, sir,' said the barman. 'How many would you like?'

'How many have you got?' asked Mel.

'Well . . . I'm not sure, sir,' said the startled barman, turning to count up his miniatures. 'It looks like 16.'

'That's perfect,' said Mel. 'We'll have the lot.'

And that's what we did. All 16 miniature bottles, four a piece, ferried back to our table on a tray.

The journey seemed to get faster and faster amidst the delicious alcohol-fuelled suspension of real life. But where Mel's mood grew steadily more benign, Sid became pedantic and competitive by turns as if he still felt the need to reassert himself after the disaster on the track. That evening the two of them went on to play a frame of snooker in a club near Mel's Talkback offices in Carnaby Street. It was a sort of grudge match with a sum partly equivalent to the afternoon's losses at stake. Sid lost and started ranting on the pavement outside the club. We left him to it and went on to dinner with other friends and then back to Mel's office with its jukebox for cigars and drinks and more drinks and reminiscences of good times and bad.

David, the conscientious best man, left before the final session of the night. But I stayed until it was light again outside. Eventually stepping out – red-eyed, skin prickling and feeling slightly mad – into the traffic and exhaust fumes of a London Friday morning.

Emma had already gone down to her parents' house in the country so I had the flat to myself for a few hours' sleep followed by a hot bath. Later Clare and David arrived to drive me off to Gloucestershire, Dave and I coyly keeping most of the details of our Haydock adventure to ourselves. Clare applied a few touches of make-up to my skin to cover up the worst of the blemishes and pockmarks that seemed to be a regular hazard of 36 hours in Mel's company.

When I arrived in Gloucestershire it was showtime. I went to bed early, got up well-slept on the Saturday morning and for the rest of that pale but sunlit winter's day managed to project a picture of health, sobriety and confidence.

Mel came to the wedding, naturally, but there weren't so many times in his company for a while after that. Mel was dangerous and there was an unspoken feeling that Mel and married life might not go together too well, at least not to begin with. But what experiences of the sporting life he'd given me to feed on . . . from Cheltenham to Newbury to Stratford to Sandown to Kempton Park. And Haydock. The coup that wasn't. But a day and night to remember.

CHAPTER SIXTEEN

It was a Monday morning in March and for me it felt like Christmas Eve. I was walking back through Gloucester, hurrying towards the featureless modern railway station on the edges of the city. The ordinary, everyday world – shoppers, bus queues, office workers buying their lunchtime sandwiches in M & S – continued all around me. Maybe they didn't know it but this was no ordinary Monday. This was Monday, 10 March 1986, and for a start there were less than 24 hours to go before the beginning of the National Hunt Festival.

I had been to do an interview in a local radio station, talking not just about horses and jockeys, odds and form but about the whole life-enhancing scale of the event that was about to take place. Thousands of racing lovers were already in the county, arriving from Ireland, Scotland, Wales, the South West, the North East, London. And thousands more were on their way. Normally I would have been chafing to join the party, to meet up with old friends and to begin the drinking and the delicious, anticipatory, pre-race speculation. But that March I had something else to be excited about, to be nervous about too, something even bigger than horse racing.

I took the train back through Stroud and on through the Golden Valley to Kemble and Swindon. Then I jumped into a cab and headed up towards Fairford on the southern edges of the Cotswolds. There had been over a month of snow and ice and a thaw had only set in the previous weekend. The weather that Monday afternoon was dry but cold with patches of snow still visible on the hillsides.

I was on my way to Mallam Waters, my mother-in-law Susie Vereker's house which was situated down a lane on a spit of land between two lakes converted from reclaimed gravel pits. Mallam was modern and Scandinavian in style with a large and stunning main room with floor-to-ceiling windows facing out across the water. It was surrounded by trees, birches and pollard willows, and the far lake beyond the garden was a bird sanctuary. The whole place had the feeling of a fabulously secluded and sophisticated hideaway and Emma and I had been hiding there for almost a month.

Like so many other couples who, in a carefree and relaxed moment, think yes, definitely, having a baby would be a fantastic idea, we'd vaguely imagined that conception would happen straightaway. And we had been puzzled, then worried, then resigned when things didn't move quite that fast. And so when, after nearly two years of that rather farcical word 'trying', we were told in the midsummer of 1985 that all was well and that Emma was indeed quite normally, naturally and healthily pregnant, we were, like millions of other expectant parents, overjoyed. The baby would arrive, so the doctors believed, some time around late February or early March of 1986. The vagueness about the date was the cause of much amusement to our friends who pointed out that if the birth was delayed to any great extent it could coincide with Cheltenham races.

Throughout the autumn and early winter we navigated our way – happily, excitedly, protectively – through the cheery doctors' visits, the more serious trips to the ante-natal clinic at the John Radcliffe Hospital in Oxford and the consideration of names, bedrooms, cots, clothes and toys. If you've been there yourself you'll know exactly what it feels like.

And then all of a sudden in mid-January, the hospital doctors announced in a worryingly casual way that there might be a 'problem'. That there could be 'complications'. And that 'conceivably' Emma, for her own and the baby's sake, would have to be admitted up to six weeks before the birth. As a result we would have to stay in reasonably close proximity to the hospital 'in case' we needed to reach it in a hurry.

Unless. Conceivably. Possibly. Have hospitals no idea how such breezy intimations of disaster strike a chill into the heart? Exactly what kind of complications were they talking about? A baby not turning round yet in the womb? That's hardly uncommon. So what else were they wary of? Emma's blood pressure? Some genetic flaw they'd spotted but weren't telling us about? We did our best to be positive but in the background there was an atmosphere of lingering unease.

Our house was in a village called Naunton, which is in a Cotswold valley by the Windrush. The roads in and out were sometimes blocked by wintry snow as was the case in February 1985 and as, in the words of Emma's younger brother David, I was 'not about to challenge Ayrton Senna for a place in the Williams Grand Prix team' (being a life-long non-driver), we moved across to Fairford, where Emma's mother was on hand to drive us to the Radcliffe when required.

As long as we were cocooned at Mallam it was possible to keep gloomy and disturbing thoughts at bay. The glamorous Susie had once run her own restaurant and she was a sensationally good cook. Her husband Stanley was generous with the wine and the whisky bottles and eating and drinking so well, albeit skipping nimbly out of the way when it seemed tactful to do so, you could almost believe the outside world wasn't there.

One topic that had certainly never played any great part in the life of the house was horse racing. My mother-in-law loves books and paintings, gardening and politics, causes, disputes and litigation. She's always been frighteningly capable with the sort of brisk, managerial style that suggests she could have run a major public company or government department. But she's never been renowned for her love of the Turf and you might say that an enthusiasm for betting and racing enjoys something of a negative approval rating in her assessment of character.

Susie's daily paper was delivered to the mailbox at the bottom of the drive. To keep myself in touch with matters on the track I'd placed an order with the newsagent in Fairford for a *Sporting Life* to be delivered too. Nobody else knew about this special arrangement or at least I didn't think they did. The papers never came until mid-morning and as long as I was in a position to walk down and pick them up personally, there was no danger of the *Life*'s existence being discovered by anyone else. Or so I thought.

One Thursday towards the end of February I was even more eager than usual to get my hands on the racing pages. The frost and ice had still not relented in Britain but it was milder in Ireland and the previous day there had been a lucrative and potentially hugely informative meeting at Thurles in County Tipperary. Amongst the runners were numerous Cheltenham prospects including the two-mile chaser Buck House, owned by Philomena Purcell, wife of the Tipperary cattle baron Seamus Purcell, and John and Sue Magnier's Knockelly Castle, at the time a highly regarded young novice hurdler trained by P.J. or 'Paddy' Prendergast Junior.

I strolled down towards the mail box around 11 a.m. only to meet my mother-in-law coming back up the drive in her Mercedes. 'Good morning, Susie,' I began cheerily as her car window slid down.

'I've got your paper,' she said handing me a crisply rolled-up copy of the *Sporting Life*.

'What?' I feigned astonishment. 'Really? But goodness. What can that be doing there? Someone in the newsagent must have thought that I . . . '

'I could've picked it up for you every day if you'd asked,' she said, her window gliding back up again. Then, with the merest hint of a smile, she drove on up to the house.

I hung around in the driveway for a moment feeling rather stupid then thought, what the hell, and fell upon the paper.

Turning to page three I discovered that Knockelly Castle had finished a promising third and that Buck House had won handily and that, yes, both horses were on course for the Festival in a fortnight's time. Assuming the weather eased sufficiently to let the meeting take place.

On that Monday morning, 10 March, the *Sporting Life* that I had bought in Gloucester along with a handful of other papers, the sports sections all well-thumbed, was packed with Festival news and prices. But as I got out of the taxi and walked up the steps into Mallam it was clear to me that racing would have to wait for a while. Emma's contractions had started. The hospital had been rung but there seemed to be no immediate alarm and she was to be checked in at five o' clock that afternoon.

Emma was smiling, nervously I thought. Looking happy, if anxious underneath, yet clearly relieved too that the weeks of pregnant discomfort were coming to an end. Susie, ever mindful of the practicalities, had organised her to tidy up the bedroom we'd been staying in. Perhaps seeing it as one final exercise of maternal control before her daughter departed to start a family of her own.

By the time we were driving into Oxford the light was fading and it was the end of a grey afternoon. There were piles of unmelted snow by the roadside and it felt more like winter than spring.

At the John Radcliffe, high on its hill looking back towards the city, all the lights were blazing. Initially things moved with a pretence of calm and with no great sense of urgency or drama. Emma was soon on a bed in a brightly lit delivery suite, a kind of windowless hotel room with doors on either side. The lighting was uncomfortably intense – we later asked them if they could dim things a little – and it was very hot. In the corner there was a large beanbag that women could choose to give birth on if they wished. Looking back it belonged in the same euphemistic world as Miriam Stoppard's jolly drawings and homoeopathic advice from women's support groups suggesting that drinking raspberry leaf tea would in itself be enough to quell the labour pains.

My evening paper, turned open at the racing page and featuring tomorrow's declared runners and riders for day one of the Festival, lay on a chair at the side of the room.

In old Westerns whenever a baby was on the way the men were always being sent off to boil more water and make pots of coffee. At the John Radcliffe the coffee came in plastic cups from a dispenser in the corridor. There was a canteen but it had closed at five o' clock.

Susie and I affected light conversation, making phoney, cheerful chat with Emma and the midwife. Gradually Emma's contractions became more frequent and more intense and the jokes dried up.

There's no room for squeamishness when a baby is coming. Men, relations and attendant supporters are speedily inducted into the basic and straightforward realities of birth. We were shown a chart which explained how far the mother's cervix had to dilate for the baby's head to emerge. When I saw how far Emma had reached and how far there was to go I winced for my beloved wife.

Susie left, politely wishing us well, and a deepening sense of reality, and of Emma being in a situation that others couldn't share, that frankly I couldn't share, took hold. She was beginning to find the pain excruciating and she kept clutching at the gas and air. If she lay on one side she felt deeply sick and no matter what she did she couldn't get comfortable. The midwives had connected her up to a machine that monitored her own and the baby's heart. To begin with the readings were fine but then after an hour or so the baby's heartbeat began to become irregular, to fluctuate and then to dip alarmingly. The explanation, as we were later to discover, was that the umbilical cord was catching around the baby's neck. The midwives and the others in the room understood the possible implications and suddenly everyone became more grave-faced and serious.

They had a fan in there now to try and ease the heat but it was still incredibly warm and things didn't feel natural or right. I couldn't believe it. This process was supposed to be so normal and straightforward and yet all of a sudden we seemed to be in the climactic scene from *A Farewell to Arms* instead of the smiling tableau on the ante-natal clinic wall.

A moustachioed young Australian doctor in a green gown and green operating theatre cap came and went, looking anxious. Then the top man, the senior obstetrician and consultant gynaecologist, was standing there too. He was also in his operating theatre gear complete with boots, his mask hanging down and blood on his gown.

The two men talked earnestly and then the Australian told us that they were going to take a blood sample from the baby. To do this they would have to insert a needle through the womb, injecting it into the top of the baby's head. I thought it sounded horrific but they seemed to feel it was both necessary and right. So I held Emma's hand once again while the Aussie, talking reassuringly all the time, took his blood test. Then he left the room in a hurry.

Emma was in a faraway place by now and for a while I left the room too and paced up and down the corridor outside. It was a desperately busy night for the hard-pressed and understaffed maternity wing and every now and then a door would open, emitting more cries of agony from within, and a doctor, nurse or midwife would run from one delivery suite to the next.

At the end of the corridor there was a little waiting-room with a couple of chairs and a telephone. I stood in there and tried to beat down the tension and fear. I had a sandwich that Susie had made me before we set out. I ate it, tasting nothing, and tried to imagine – and not to imagine – what it would be like if we lost the baby. What uplifting thing could I say to Emma? Where would we go, what would we do and how would we get over it?

Rehearsing the scene in my mind, yet simultaneously not wanting to, I went back into the delivery suite. At that very moment the young Australian houseman rushed back in through the other door. He gave us a big grin and a thumbs-up sign. 'Fine healthy baby,' he yelled. 'Fine healthy baby. But now we're going to get him out.' Underneath his relief and encouragement there was no mistaking the urgency of the situation. The baby was, as yet, fine and healthy but if the impeded labour continued much longer the possibility of brain damage to the child and even a haemorrhage for his mother was very real.

And that's when the delivery room suddenly filled up with people, all arriving in a hurry and all focused on Emma for, as the Australian had said, they just wanted to get the baby out fast. And that's what they did in a scene of exhilarating yet frightening drama. The Aussie leading the way. Talking, encouraging, urging, joking, for one last half an hour. Emma pouring sweat, her face contorted, midwives at her shoulder, pushing, pushing. Until finally at around 11 that evening little Jack – we knew if it was a boy we'd call him Jack – entered the world.

At the last the Aussie seemed to whip him out with a flourish, as if he was literally producing a rabbit from a hat. A long, slippery fellow, he was thrust into his ecstatic mother's arms. Then as poor ravaged Emma was attended to by the brilliant life-saving young Australian doctor, Jack was cleaned off and wrapped up and given to me to hug and hold and talk to gently. The lights mercifully softer now but even so Jack's blue eyes blinking at these bewildering new surroundings. He was put in a little crib at the foot of the bed for weighing, measuring and other details. He weighed 7 lb 10 oz with the typical newly born baby's Churchillian appearance. We were told that he'd been slightly overcooked from being more than a week overdue and that he'd actually lost weight in the womb towards the end of the pregnancy. Seventeen years later he weighs more like 13 stone and is over 6 ft tall. He's still got blue eyes though and, like his 15-year-old younger brother, he's a joy to be with.

Nurses came and went cleaning up the debris. This again was no time or place for the squeamish and the floor was liberally splattered with blood and tissue. The brilliant young Australian performed one last task, sewing up Emma as sensitively as he could, before dashing off to deliver somebody else's baby.

Emma and I were offered a cup of tea and frankly at that moment nothing could've tasted sweeter or felt more appropriately and hearteningly British. My body was still numb from the tension and excitement but the dominant feeling was one of enormous and overwhelming relief. It had happened. We'd had a baby. We hadn't lost him. It hadn't ended in the unimaginable anguish of a stillborn tragedy. Death had been averted. He was here. He was real. He was very much alive and well. We had done it. Emma had done it. And I was a father like my father before me. The future had arrived.

CHAPTER SEVENTEEN

The hospital porters came – porters like I had been at Pembury on my 18-year-old weekends, 14 years before – and they wheeled Emma's bed, with Emma holding Jack, into the lift and on up to the ward. It was long after midnight now and the lights were low but all around us there were the muffled sounds of other mothers and babies, other parcels of joy and concern.

Jack was hungry. Emma was shattered and in urgent need of sleep. As the baby cuddled up to his mother's bosom he would occasionally clench his hands and then fling them out instinctively. I left them eventually, already excited about seeing them both again the following day. But I was not about to go back to my mother-in-law's house in Fairford. Not now. And I was not going all the way home to Naunton either. So where to stay in Oxford at 1.30 a.m. the night before the start of Cheltenham races? Well, I had the great good fortune to meet a cab driver outside the John Radcliffe who happened to know of a hotel that had had a cancellation. It was the Linton Lodge: comfortable, medium to top range in Linton Road not far from the Banbury Road in that residential north Oxford enclave popular with dons and ever-divorcing novelists. And the perfect touch, the clincher in the most appropriate way, was that the Linton Lodge was owned by Ladbrokes.

When I arrived the lights were still on in the bar and restaurant. I was desperate for a drink and ordered a large Remy Martin. The barman then obligingly hastened off to fix me a snack.

There was still one group of diners sitting at their table, all of them clearly happy and replete after a good evening. Conversation, racing conversation, flowing like the brandy. And every voice an Irish one. They invited me to join them. It was the eve of the Cheltenham Festival and normally I'd have been thrilled just to talk to them about horses. But my wife had just had a baby and that night I was unable to conceal my excitement and needed to share the moment with others. When I told them my news, that we had had a child, our first, a son, their response was magical. They clapped me on the back and shook me by the hand. Toasts were proposed. They drank to my health and Jack's and Emma's. Cigars were handed round, champagne sent for. And between us we drank the night away.

Some time after dawn I crawled upstairs for a few hours' sleep. When I awoke it was to a beautiful spring day, the greyness and snow of the previous afternoon and evening all gone. I rang my mother and father to tell them about Jack and I rang Susie and Stanley and Emma's sister Jane and a few others. By this time I was ravenous and I followed my nose downstairs, led by the delicious smells of coffee, bacon and woodsmoke. There was an open fire burning in the foyer and plumes of dust were held in the sunlight that was flowing in through the French windows.

My Irish friends were all up, all looking staggeringly well and all seated round the table, a *Sporting Life* to hand, and tackling everything that breakfast could throw at them. I joined them again enthusiastically and over the sausages, bacon, eggs and black pudding and the pots of coffee and the cigarettes we went through the first day's Festival card.

Everyone agreed that See You Then, trained in Lambourn by Nicky Henderson and victorious in the Champion Hurdle the previous year, was a banker bet to win the race for the second year running. He had the class. He had the speed. Gaye Brief, the winner in 1983, was too old to do it again, though he might run into a place. The others were handicappers.

But what about the first race, the Supreme Novices Hurdle, I asked? It had no fewer than 29 runners. Deep Idol, who had won that race at Thurles a fortnight before, was expected to start favourite. But then there was Canute Express, a winner at Chepstow only the previous Saturday and trained by Homer 'The Business' Scott, a young and, at the time, very much a happening Irish trainer who'd landed some mighty gambles for his roguish owners that winter. And then there was Knockelly Castle, only third to Deep Idol that February afternoon but universally expected to be a lot sharper now. 'Now he would be a serious horse,' said one of my breakfast companions, dropping his voice and adopting an appropriately reverential and respectful tone.

They all agreed it would be a wonderful thing if your man Paddy Prendergast, P.J. Junior, son of the great Paddy Prendergast – Irish flat-racing trainer number one before Vincent O'Brien – were to train a Cheltenham winner. But could he? He had the looks for it. He was tall and charismatic with swept-back hair and eyes like Robert Mitchum. He was witty. He was droll. He was a horse dealer to his fingertips. But could he train a Festival winner? He'd had fancied runners before, but no winners.

In the saddle this time would be Frank Berry, who'd won the Gold Cup on Glencaraig Lady in 1972 and had given that superb ride to Bobsline in the Arkle against Noddy's Ryde in 1984. 'Frank will do the job,' the Irishman assured me. 'There'll be no problem.' Maybe not. But I couldn't help feeling that with 28 horses to beat around Prestbury Park, the inexperienced Knockelly Castle, who'd had just the two hurdle races in his life, would have to be every bit as special as P.J. said he was.

I left them discussing the tricky three-mile handicap hurdle that closed the Tuesday programme. They were as obsessed about racing as I was but that morning I was even more excited about getting back to the John Radcliffe to see Emma and Jack.

I hurried down to the shops in Summertown to buy a few things that Emma had requested and then took a taxi up to Headington. Emma was recovering slowly but was still very tender. The baby was continuing his little hand gestures, clenching then flexing his fingers. Now there were a new set of things for his parents to learn about and work out, like breastfeeding and changing nappies as the very real and joyful but exhausting reality of life with a small baby sank in.

Susie came to visit and meet her first grandson. She was looking very smart and was off to meet Stanley afterwards as she felt he deserved some attention after we'd been cluttering up his house for a month. She'd brought champagne and flowers and there were numerous telegrams to open. As Susie left she humorously if mercilessly teased us about the many sleep-deprived nights we had to look forward to.

Around lunchtime the baby fell asleep and Emma too was longing to rest, but she asked me not to go too far away as she wanted me to be there when she woke up again. That was absolutely fine by me but as the clock ticked on past two o' clock the televised racing was, of course, about to begin. So would there be any chance of watching it?

There was a television at the end of the ward but numerous expectant mothers were gathered round it watching an afternoon soap opera. There was about as much chance of me persuading them to switch over to horse racing as there would've been of selling Mrs Thatcher a CND cookbook. Then I remembered I'd seen a TV in the small room on the labour ward one floor below. I made my way down there, which was easy in those pre-security-conscious days, walking past the closed doors of the delivery suites from where more groans and cries of agony could be heard.

The little room at the end of the corridor was empty. I switched on the television set. It was very old and black and white but it was tuned to BBC 1. And there suddenly was the aforementioned Paddy Prendergast Junior talking to Peter O'Sullevan on the gallops that morning in what was obviously a pre-recorded interview. 'Is he ready, Paddy?' O'Sullevan had asked, obviously meaning Knockelly Castle. 'Peter . . . he's as cocked and ready as a cowboy's gun,' replied the trainer. 'If I don't win with this one I never will.' Then they cut back to the 29 runners wheeling around at the start in the spring sunshine. Knockelly Castle, named after a picturesque ruin in a field bordering John Magnier's Coolmore Stud, was joint favourite with Deep Idol. The tapes went up, O'Sullevan's voice went up with them and another Festival meeting was underway.

As the field streamed past the winning post on the first circuit a nursing sister walked past the room. She paused, looked in, saw a man watching racing on the television, frowned and walked on. A few moments later, as the horses approached the hill on the far side of the course, I heard a door open to a delivery suite and the piteous cries of a woman in labour. The sister walked past again. This time she was positively glaring. I could feel her thinking, 'There's a man, a typical chauvinistic man, watching, yes, watching horse racing while his partner's in agony.' I wanted to speak out in my defence. 'It's not what you think,' I'd have said. 'We had our baby last night. They're both upstairs asleep. But there is this thing called the Cheltenham Festival . . . '

The race was nearly over now. Frank Berry must've thought he was riding a cross between the great Champion Hurdler Sea Pigeon and Nijinsky because for the first half of the contest he'd held up Knockelly Castle in third to last place. The combination started to make ground on the uphill run on the far side but their momentum was checked by tiring horses dropping back. They made headway racing down the hill but as they rounded the home turn they still had plenty to do. And they didn't do it. The shock winner was a 66–1 outsider River Ceiriog, representing the See You Then team of Nicky Henderson and Steve Smith Eccles. Deep Idol was second. Knockelly, running on strongly but too late, finished fourth. And Canute Express was fifth. No luck for P.J. but lucky for me. If I'd have been there I'd have done my money.

Emma and Jack were still asleep 40 minutes later so I just

managed to catch a glimpse of the Arkle Trophy, watching it on the ward TV this time, and saw Oregon Trail, trained in Lambourn by Simon Christian, come home the 14–1 winner. Desert Orchid, by no means a champion at Cheltenham in those days, finished third.

Miraculously Emma and Jack were still asleep as the hour drew nigh for the Champion Hurdle. I'd backed See You Then, telephoning my wager through to a local bookie in the country. I had to see the race somehow. Up on the ward the expectant mums were all back in force and glued to *Emmerdale Farm*. There seemed no alternative to going back down to the little room with the black and white television on the floor below.

I practically tiptoed along the corridor, reached the TV room undetected and switched on the set. The runners were at the post. In the final show See You Then was 5–6 favourite with Gaye Brief on 14–1, and 20–1 bar. The runners and riders made a line. 'And they're under starter's orders for the 1986 Waterford Crystal Champion Hurdle,' declared O'Sullevan, '. . . and they're off.' I could hear the customary great cheer from the crowd even on the inadequate TV.

I think Robin Wonder led over the first two flights from Stan's Pride with Gaye Brief in third and See You Then tracking them in about sixth place. As they swept up past the grandstand and turned left out into the country, I was aware that somebody else was in the room. 'I don't know much about horse racing myself,' said a voice. I turned round to see a man, maybe in his late 30s, sitting awkwardly on the chair by the door. He was twisting his fingers around nervously. 'Really?' I replied, trying to ignore him as politely as possible. 'No. I'm more of a football man.' 'Are you?' I said tetchily. 'Well, this a very important race. One of the most important of the year.' I tried to turn the sound up. The horses had just met the rising ground and were starting to climb the hill on the far side of the track.

'Do you live this way?' asked the man. 'Not exactly,' I replied as See You Then moved into fourth place. 'We're Abingdon ourselves,' said the man. 'Though we do most of our shopping in

Oxford. But we try to avoid Saturdays. Well, you've got to, haven't you?' 'I suppose you have,' I agreed, my voice cracking. At that moment I didn't really care if he did his shopping in Reykjavik, I just wanted to watch the climax of the Champion Hurdle. I turned the volume up again. The sound boomed out embarrassingly. The sister reappeared in the doorway looking furious. I turned the sound down again. She sighed and went away. I turned it back up just a little. 'And they've got two flights left to jump,' called O'Sullevan. 'And it's the old champion Gaye Brief who goes on. Robin Wonder in second. And See You Then absolutely cantering on the heels of the leaders.' 'Go on, Steve. Go on, See You Then,' I cried.

'My wife went into labour at nine o' clock this morning,' said the man, clearly desperate to talk. 'They say it could be hours yet.' I shot him a look. He was gazing at the wall above the television, fingers still twisting. 'I . . . I'm really sorry,' I stumbled. On the TV screen they'd rounded the home turn. Gaye Brief was on the inside and See You Then was drawing level on the stands side. 'But look . . . just look at this. This is a top horse . . . a really top-class racehorse.'

'And Steve Smith Eccles shakes him up and the champion goes on,' continued O'Sullevan. 'He's five, six, seven lengths clear. He's out on his own. See You Then wins the Champion Hurdle.' I punched the air, then immediately felt sheepish and turned the volume right down. I looked back at my companion. 'Do you win often?' he asked. He was trying to smile. 'Not often enough,' I said smiling back. There was an awkward pause. 'This is our third,' he said. 'They've all been a nightmare. We don't seem to have much luck.' 'They're very good here,' I said. 'Honestly. The doctors are wonderful. I'm sure your wife will be fine. I'm sure the baby will be fine.' He nodded, unconvinced. We sat there a bit longer, watching See You Then returning to unsaddle and his owner being presented with the trophy, the sound still down. Then he went back to his wife and I went back upstairs to the maternity ward, where Emma and Jack had just woken up.

Later that day we received a visit from the senior obstetrician, the top man who'd appeared in the delivery suite the previous night in his operating theatre cap, gown and boots. Now he was in his pinstripe mufti, God of the ward, sister and a staff nurse in respectful attendance. He peered shyly at Emma and Jack from behind his half-moon glasses, looking like a restrained version of Kenneth Williams as Dr Tinkle in a *Carry On* film. 'We were very worried about you last night, you know,' he said quietly. 'We thought we might lose you both.' It made me shudder to think of it. To recall the heat, the trauma, the pain and anxiety on Emma's face and the sight of the Australian sticking a needle into our unborn baby's head. And it made me feel ashamed that I hadn't been more supportive of the other anxious father in the television room downstairs.

Two and a half years later our second son was born in the same building on a sunny September day. No bright lights. No overheating. A healthy, natural labour with just two midwives and barely a white coat in sight. The comparison with the drama of 10 March 1986 would be hard to exaggerate. But what a lesson learned. Even in Western Europe in the late twentieth century, childbirth could be fatal.

Wednesday's routine was very similar to Tuesday's. I had breakfast in the hotel with my new racing friends and once again we compared notes on the Cheltenham card. The Irish punters assured me that Homer Scott's Omerta couldn't lose the four-mile National Hunt Chase for amateur riders. They also felt the good ground might enable Buck House to beat the favourite Bobsline in the Queen Mother Champion Chase. I thought Fulke Walwyn's strapping great hurdler Ten Plus was a banker in the opening race.

The sun was shining as I set off for the John Radcliffe. The daffodils were out and the spring-like atmosphere was infectious. Another day in a maternity ward with a two-day-old son suddenly seemed the most natural thing in the world and the easiest to cope with. Emma and Jack settled down for a rest a little later than they had on Tuesday afternoon but while they were asleep I was naturally hoping I might be able to watch a race or two.

The ward television was monopolised again by the expectant mothers and a quick reconnoitre of the delivery suites below convinced me I couldn't return to the small sitting-out room down the corridor. The atmosphere was too fraught with midwives and doctors rushing in and out, the air torn by women's dreadful screams. So I went out into nearby Headington and found a Ladbrokes office on the London Road.

It was a doubly important week for bookmakers because the Conservative Home Secretary Douglas Hurd had chosen the Cheltenham Festival as the moment to permit a modest relaxation of the gaming laws. TV had been allowed in betting shops for the very first time along with Gents' and Ladies' lavatories and permission to serve Styrofoam cups of instant coffee and the odd biscuit or Mars Bar.

I could just imagine the stiff-necked Hurd explaining his innovations in Cabinet much like a Governor or senior staff member of the Judd School. 'The new privileges could not be taken for granted.' 'They might be extended but they might just as easily be withdrawn at any time if behaviour didn't match up to appropriate standards' etc. etc.

Hurd's liberalisation at least enabled a large crowd of us shiftless Ladbrokes customers to watch the BBC's Cheltenham pictures that Wednesday and to listen to O'Sullevan's commentary as Ten Plus won the SunAlliance Hurdle at 5–2 and Buck House, given a beautiful ride by Tommy Carmody, strode three lengths clear in the two-mile championship. His starting price was also 5–2 and I'd started the day with a double.

Later that afternoon I took a bus up into the centre of the city to do some more shopping for Emma. It was still mild and sunny and the streets were bustling with people enjoying the unaccustomed luxury of walking around without coats and scarves after the long weeks of snow and icy weather.

I went into Jim Bailey's betting office, which was up a flight of stairs off Cornmarket. I'd gone there often as a student and nothing much had changed. The BBC Cheltenham coverage had finished so, in this era before satellite racing transmissions began, it was back to gazing at the tannoy in the corner and listening to the dulcet tones of the Extel, or Exchange Telegraph, commentator.

The National Hunt Chase, which at the time was the penultimate race on the Wednesday programme, started at around ten to five. There were 22 runners with Omerta, whose jockey Mr Lorcan Wyer was a proper Irish amateur, meaning the equivalent of many professionals in England, the 9–4 favourite.

It takes at least 8 minutes for 22 horses to complete a 4-mile steeplechase at Cheltenham and in the Extel days with their frequent interruptions, even of such a prestige meeting, for dog shows from Monmore and Hackney, it felt like even longer. For the first seven and a half minutes that March afternoon there wasn't a single, solitary mention of Omerta. And as the leaders were described racing towards the penultimate fence, I felt like a fool who'd jumped onto a talking-horse bandwagon. Then came a terse but sweet comment from the Extel man with the nasal voice. 'And beginning to make significant headway now on the outside of the field is number 14 . . . Omerta.' Yes. Oh yes. He was making significant headway alright. Quietly but expertly ridden by Lorcan Wyer (who did indeed turn professional soon afterwards), he had everything covered. He jumped the second-last upsides, according to the commentator, then took up the running and went right away. This banker had landed and I'd backed three winners in a single day at the National Hunt Festival. Two of them favourites, maybe, but a winner is a winner all the same.

Back in the hospital that spring evening there were more visitors to see Emma and Jack, including Emma's sister Jane, and more practice for me at changing and nursing our two-day-old son. Emma was totally exhausted and that night a kind but firm staff nurse insisted that Jack should be wheeled off to the nursery for a few hours so that his mother could rest properly without him waking her continually and demanding more food. As I left

I saw him through the window next to the nursing station. Lying in his crib, blinking and peering about him, and seemingly wondering where the party had gone.

The following day, Thursday, 13 March, was the third and final day of the National Hunt Festival with the 64th running of the Cheltenham Gold Cup as its climax. And it had been agreed with my generous and tolerant wife that I would go racing.

I left Emma and Jack with the staff nurse and with a visit from her younger brother and set off shortly after 11 with my best and most indispensable Cheltenham companion, David Tupman, who'd been commuting up from London. Thirty years on from our first Festival expedition, David's become a prosperous and successful antique dealer, working long hours to support a family, but he's still gambling. Always gambling. And like his friend, he's retained a religious devotion to the annual rites of March.

CHAPTER EIGHTEEN

Thursday had dawned dry and mild, albeit greyer and mistier than the previous two days and with no sunshine. Tupman had brought a bottle of champagne to the hospital for Emma and another that we opened in the car. We drank it heading west along the A40. Eynsham, Witney, Burford: the anticipation growing by the mile.

David knew every short cut, every back road and narrow country lane. Avoiding the direct route into Cheltenham via Charlton Kings, we dropped off the Bourton to Andoversford road near Aylworth Farm and carried on through Guiting Power and out past Roel Gate and Guiting Wood towards Winchcombe. Ten minutes later we had breasted the top of Cleeve Hill and could see the racecourse down below, the white tented pavilions and corporate marquees arrayed around the stands like some medieval, military encampment.

Up until this point we'd been lucky with the traffic but now we hit the queues. Coaches, cars and taxis. Bentleys, Range Rovers, Jags and Mercs all crawling down the Cheltenham side of the hill. 'To hell with this,' said Tupman, dropping right down the precipitous lane that leads through Woodmancote and continues past a school and through a housing estate and then onwards through the fields behind Southam. We came out by the old railway bridge on the slip road near the bottom entrance to the racecourse. As we nudged forward the last few hundred yards the helicopters were sweeping in overhead and the whirring of the blades was like the churning, nervous excitement in my stomach.

Out on the grass in the Members' car park smartly dressed men and women were gathered round car boots and eating picnics standing up. The pâté and the game pie, the soup and the sloe gin being handed round by agreeable hosts. 'I say, Rupert. Your dog's gone and eaten my vol-au-vent.'

'Has he really? Good old Bowser. Isn't he a character?'

There were men in velvet-collar coats. City men. County men. Chinless men. Tall, commanding, thrusting men. Fox-hunting men. There were horsey women. Brisk, no-nonsense women. And seriously high-maintenance trophy women, their husbands desirable not simply for the size of their bank accounts but also because of their frequent absences on work, leaving the wives plenty of free time to entertain younger gents with experience in the saddle.

As we walked up towards the grandstand, loudspeaker announcements drifted back towards us on the breeze. A giant blimp hovered in the sky and a biplane trailing a newspaper advert flew back and forth like some potential agent of disaster in a Hitchcock film.

We joined the groups of racegoers filing patiently past the gatemen, the necessary badges flapping on our lapels, as always on an English racecourse, as if we'd all just won a prize at an agricultural show. There were men in coats and caps. Bareheaded men. Men in wax jackets. Irish men in suits and ties. Handsome, quick-witted men. Hair swept back, cigarettes in hands and a thick wedge of notes in their trouser pockets. And nearly all of them clasping a *Sporting Life* or a *Racing Post* just as Tupman and I were.

Once inside we paused to buy a Timeform race card and were then swept up quickly in the huge, jostling crowd. The buzz of conversation humming in our ears. David and the rest of our friends, like at least 50 per cent of the other racegoers present, had been here each day. They'd had time to settle in, to re-acquaint themselves and get used to the electric but exhausting Festival atmosphere. I was back for the first time in 12 months and, with the first race little more than 20 minutes away, I needed to acclimatise fast.

I fought my way out onto the terrace close to the rails bookies and the betting ring and looked out across the course at the lush green turf, at the fences and hurdles, spruce and ready, at the white-painted running rail and at Cleeve Hill rising up in the background. I looked back behind me at the crowds packed into all three storeys of the stand and at the punters battling their way in and out of Tatts and I breathed in those familiar racetrack smells – there were fewer fast-food kiosks 17 years ago – crushed grass, champagne and cigar smoke. And I felt as if I'd put my head inside a bell jar and inhaled the strongest and most pungent narcotic. It was as intoxicating to me at that moment as any joint or opium pipe and I could feel it tugging at me like an underwater current. It was time to catch up, to bet, to drink, to play, to let go, but I was also a father now with new and exhilarating responsibilities. So I would have to ease into the experience gently. Savouring it step by step, one race at a time.

The 28 runners for the first, the *Daily Express* Triumph Hurdle, were coming out onto the course. The Triumph is a Grade One championship contest for four year olds and Express newspapers sponsored it from 1965 to 1996. Nowadays it's sponsored by JCB and boasts total prize money of £100,000. Past winners have included one or two truly great horses, like Persian War and Night Nurse, who both went on to be champion hurdlers, and a fair number of other animals who subsequently vanished into obscurity.

In 1973, the first year I was actually there at Cheltenham on Gold Cup day, Captain Ryan Price saddled the winner. Moonlight Bay, a classy ex-flat racing type, was ridden by the great hurdle race stylist Johnny Haine and returned the 85–40 favourite. The Captain, a punter of inspired rascality, greeted his victory with a typical display of suave braggadocio, promising that Moonlight Bay would win everything from the following year's Champion Hurdle to the 1974 Prix de l'Arc De Triomphe. It didn't quite work out that way but then the Captain was never a man for understatement.

Other Triumph winners have gone off at 25–1, 66–1 and even 80–1 and, in short, this is not generally regarded as the sort of race to have your shirt, trousers and pants on.

I decided that with the ground still riding good or good to fast I needed a Moonlight Bay, a horse with a touch of flat-racing speed rather than a slugger, and ended up going each way on Son Of Ivor, who was trained on the Curragh by Dermot Weld. A top flat-racing trainer and ground-breaking winner of big races overseas, Weld nearly won the Grand National twice with Greasepaint. It also helped that Son Of Ivor was to be ridden by Tommy Carmody, who had won the Champion Chase on Buck House on the Wednesday and who, in the late 1970s and early '80s, was as good a jockey round Prestbury Park as anyone riding at the time. Son Of Ivor went off at 16–1.

I remember few details of the race. There was no giant screen in front of the stands at Cheltenham in 1986. You watched through your binoculars and listened to the racecourse commentator, who would once have been the splendidly named Cloudsley Marsham or Michael Seth-Smith and then became Robin Gray or Jim McGrath or, on non-Channel 4 days, Graham Goode. And, gradually, the indistinct blur of colours, shapes, silks and horseflesh resolved itself into an outcome.

All the races at Cheltenham on Gold Cup day take place on the so-called New Course and there's a very long run from the second-last hurdle to the final flight. Rounding the home turn it looked as if any one of half-a-dozen horses might win but over the last it was the 40–1 outsider Solar Cloud, ridden by Peter Scudamore and trained locally by David Nicholson, who hit the front. In a desperate finish he held on by three-quarters of a length from Terry Ramsden's Brunico. My selection Son Of Ivor seemed to come from nowhere in the final furlong and ran on strongly to be a short head away third.

I had at least won on the each way part of my bet and while most punters weren't exactly beside themselves with joy it was an emotional moment for Nicholson and Scudamore, each of them enjoying their first ever Festival success.

Scudamore, the epitome of a decent, hard-working professional, went on to set as then unimaginable numerical records with Martin Pipe but he always lacked the charisma of an arrogant chancer and genius like John Francome or a popular hero like Jonjo O'Neill.

As for Nicholson – racing nickname The Duke – he'd been trying and failing to saddle a winner at the March meeting for years and Solar Cloud's odds were a reflection of the bookies' faith in his prospects. Tupman, like many regular punters, had a certain view of the man and would always remember the day at Sandown in November 1980 when Nicholson's good hurdler Broadsword was somehow beaten by a 50–1 outsider called Lir, who achieved nothing in any future races. David unwisely reinvested on Broadsword in the 1981 Triumph and again in the following season's Champion Hurdle but Broadsword – game but fatally one-paced – finished second both times.

In fairness Nicholson went on to train a string of Festival winners in the late '80s and early '90s and Richard Dunwoody – a candidate along with Francome and Tony McCoy for the title of the greatest jump jockey ever – gifted him a Gold Cup triumph with Charter Party in 1988. The Duke was a horseman – he rode Mill House in the '67 Gold Cup after all – and riders like Scudamore, Dunwoody and Adrian Maguire all thrived under his guidance. By the mid-'90s his nickname, originally coined during his riding days and a reference to his lordly manner in the weighing-room, seemed past its sell-by date. But, in spite of his somewhat bullying tendencies, the public still warmed to his passionate love of the Turf and loyalty to those who'd been loyal to him.

The Duke is an ardent supporter of fox-hunting and anyone who takes the view that it's fundamentally illiberal to ban an activity just because you don't like the people who participate in it, might find themselves in an unlikely alliance with him. Of course it's not necessary to be a hunting enthusiast to enjoy jump racing or betting on jumping. It's probably not even inevitable that without hunting there'd be no point-to-point racing or amateur riders' steeplechases, but anyone with any sense of racing history must surely recognise the sport's umbilical link with the elemental passion of the chase. Certainly anyone who grew up with memories such as I have, of the Old Surrey and Burstow, the Eridge and the Southdown, or anyone who has been racing on a Sunday in Ireland on some gloriously wild and frozen hilltop in Cork or Westmeath will understand point-to-pointing and hunter chasing's peculiar yet addictive allure.

It's fair to say that long-suffering betting-shop punters, many of them from towns and cities, tend to be suspicious of all amateur rider contests and to regard the Corinthians as licensed buffoons. Admittedly even the best amateur rider races – and the Christies Foxhunters' at Cheltenham and the corresponding event at Liverpool are the best in the calendar – are rarely as compelling as watching Messrs McCoy, Walsh and Williamson, but they are often a lot more exciting than witnessing 20 maiden two year olds scrambling up the straight mile at Newmarket. And the canniest gamblers know that in an amateur riders' steeplechase, where all the pilots are risking their necks for the gas of it, it's sometimes easier to pick a winner than when the professionals are in action.

The rule is simple. Back the best jockey in the field. English and Irish trainers are always fighting to get the services of the same three or four men and more often than not the best rider will be teamed with the best horse or at least with the horse with the best chance of winning. And while there have been many brave and talented amateurs in the ranks of English Corinthians from Lord Mildmay to Johnny Oaksey and Gentleman Jim Wilson, they are mostly not within a country mile of their Irish equivalents.

Top professionals like Ruby Walsh, Paul Carberry and Norman Williamson all rode as amateurs and in point-to-points in their early days and Carberry, for one, remains a totally fearless man to hounds when he's got a few days off or a winter holiday from the stewards.

Carberry, Walsh and Williamson, so far from being in the Pat Taaffe mould, are as polished and stylish as any jump jockeys in the history of the game. Ruby's father Ted, now long since become a Grand National-winning trainer and RTE commentator, was never exactly stylish but back between the '70s and the mid-1980s he was the toughest and most capable amateur rider on either side of the Irish Sea. Prior to 1986 Ted had ridden three Festival winners and he could always be relied upon to give you a run for your money, including, in those less sensitive times, doing what was necessary with his whip if victory was in the balance.

In the 1986 Christies Foxhunters' Chase, the second race of the Cheltenham Thursday programme, Ted was riding a horse called Attitude Adjuster, owned, like Knockelly Castle, by Sue Magnier and trained by her Tipperary neighbour Michael 'Mouse' Morris, successful with Buck House the previous day. Mouse – long hair curling over his coat collar and a fag permanently in his hand – was himself a leading jump jockey, both amateur and then professional, and like Paul Carberry he's still an enthusiastic horseman over a natural run of country. But Mouse Morris is also a rather different kind of Irishman to Ted Walsh and certainly a lot less garrulous.

Mouse is technically the Honourable Michael Morris and his father was Lord Killanin, former President of the International Olympic Committee. Mouse's brother Redmond is a film producer and he worked with Neil Jordan on *Michael Collins*, *Interview With A Vampire* and *The Butcher Boy*.

Mouse was sent to Ampleforth, the Catholic public school in Yorkshire, where he enjoyed a relationship with the authorities that sounded very similar to my own with F.H. Taylor and Co. Morris ended up leaving early 'by mutual agreement' and going back to his native Ireland to ride horses. As an amateur he was attached to Edward O'Grady's gambling stable at Ballynonty in

County Tipperary and in 1974 he was on board Mr Midland for the O'Grady team when, like Omerta, it landed a mighty plunge in the National Hunt Chase.

Mouse also rode Gay Future on O'Grady's gallops, preparing the Tony Murphy-owned hurdler for the most famous and uplifting of all betting coups at Cartmel on August Bank Holiday Monday, 1974. When the police came to lift Murphy, John Horgan, O'Grady and other co-conspirators at Cheltenham's Queen's Hotel on the eve of the 1975 Festival meeting, Morris was also on their list of suspects. But Mouse – slow-burning, quick-witted Mouse – got away. Tucked up in the boot of Robert Sangster's car. To ask him about the story is to get a typically dry and poker-faced response. 'You can just say I was mentioned in despatches,' he says.

Interviews with the man always involve a lot of talking by the questioner. The trainer, most likely to be in jeans and cowboy boots, fixes you with a look, half-smiling like Lester Piggott, as if to say, 'I suspect you of being an idiot and nothing you've said so far has persuaded me otherwise.'

Mouse is a passionate devotee of the National Hunt Festival. 'What's your favourite racecourse?' you ask him. 'Cheltenham, Cheltenham, Cheltenham,' he replies, gazing into the middle distance. He won the 1975 Champion Chase on Skymas and right from the start of his training career he wanted to have horses good enough to run there.

In 1979 he nearly pulled off a colossal punt in the County Hurdle with a gelding called Roadway, who was owned by the Horgan brothers and beaten a short head in a photo-finish. Then in 1983 he sent over Buck House to win the Supreme Novices Hurdle for the Purcell family. As Tommy Carmody went clear up the Cheltenham hill a winning punter threw her hat up high into the air near the finishing line. A copy of the *Sporting Life* sailed up after it and Mouse Morris, trainer, was on the Festival scoreboard.

Things haven't gone so well for Mouse, either personally or professionally, in recent years but in the mid-'80s he was the coming man. In 1984 Buck House finished third in the Champion Hurdle. A year after that he was runner-up in the Arkle Trophy and then in March '86 came the Champion Chase. Mouse wasn't finished for the meeting yet either. In the Foxhunters' he was running this six-year-old character of a horse, this Attitude Adjuster, whose owner Sue Magnier is herself an accomplished horsewoman as befits a daughter of Vincent O'Brien.

Attitude Adjuster had been hunted with the 'Tipps' or Tipperary Foxhounds that winter. He was considered talented but quirky. A horse 'with a mind of his own', as the form books say. Or 'has ability but not always inclined to put it in'. Meaning he's inclined to be a shirker at the business end of a race. Mouse had just the plan for him. He'd booked Ted Walsh. No horse would hold out on Ted. Like Mr Creakle in *David Copperfield*, he'd get the measure of them. For sure he would.

The combination had already won the Coolmore-sponsored hunter chase at that same informative Thurles meeting that had featured Knockelly Castle and Deep Idol and Buck House in the P.Z. Mower Chase. The British bookmakers were sceptical not only of Attitude Adjuster's attitude but also of his jumping ability and they'd priced him up at 10–1. Yet Ted Walsh was in such a different class to the other jockeys and Mouse Morris so obviously in form, his runners fit and firing, that I thought . . . why not? He has to be worth another each way interest.

He won thrillingly by a neck. And what a skilful and determined ride Ted gave him. He kept him up with the leaders all the way. Settled him into a rhythm. Gave him a good view of his fences. Asked him to stand off and leap in a way the young horse probably never imagined he could and then what a finish he rode too. Where one had wincingly feared he might be merciless with his whip. Thrashing Attitude Adjuster up the hill in a style thankfully seen less on racecourses in recent years. But not a bit of it. He never laid a stroke on his mount. Never even picked up his stick in anger. It was all coaxing, driving, urging, riding. Hands, heels. Rhythm, rhythm. Horse and man. Attitude

Adjuster, renowned for putting his head in the air and looking round for ways to lose, responded heroically and the duo crossed the line to a crescendo of noise.

There were the usual memorable scenes of Irish celebration in the unsaddling enclosure. Mouse, in his blue coat, was grinning broadly and lighting his 21st cigarette of the day. Sue Magnier and her husband John and the Nagles and the Horgans and other members of what was becoming the Coolmore Mafia were all on hand. And as for Ted, well Ted – who immediately announced his retirement from the saddle – was fêted. And many were the compliments for his restrained riding style. But it seems we had all missed something, or so the stories go, as one journalist, congratulating Ted for his unexpected kindness at the finish, received this perhaps apocryphal and misquoted response. 'Ah well,' says Ted. 'The fucker doesn't do a stitch for the whip. But if I'd thought he'd have run for it . . . I'd have cut rashers off him.'

As the presentations for the Foxhunters' began, the giant trophy handed over to the fetching Sue M., the clock was ticking on. And suddenly the runners and riders for the Gold Cup itself appeared on the electronic board at the far end of the paddock. Everything on a big day's Festival racing seems to move with increasing speed towards the main event. Each new scene was building on the drama of the preceding one, leaving the spectators with no time to watch and bet and cheer and drink and go to the lavatory and see the runners for the next race saddle up. You can only do one or two of these things at most.

I would've liked to see the Gold Cup runners in the more intimate surroundings of the pre-parade ring but by 3.10 they were all on their way to the main paddock. Racegoers already packed onto the terraces, straining to look over people's heads or fighting their way down the overcrowded aisles like rabbits burrowing into the undergrowth.

I love these final minutes. The crowd is never more expectant and the horses with their owners, trainers and jockeys are brought together at last. Still apart, just, but in full sight of one another and the racecourse beyond. We have all waited months for this. Just as earlier generations waited for Arkle and Mill House, for Golden Miller and Cottage Rake. I wasn't moving out now. The cathartic event of Thursday, 13 March – not a four-year-old hurdle race or a hunter chase but the Blue Riband steeplechase of the sport – was about to begin.

CHAPTER NINETEEN

There were 11 runners lining up for a first prize of £54,900. Ten of them were trained in England. One in Ireland.

Foremost among the home representatives was Forgive 'N' Forget, who had won the Gold Cup impressively 12 months before. Forgive 'N' Forget almost qualified as Irish. He was owned by an Irishman, Tim Kilroe, and trained in Yorkshire by the Tipperary-born Jimmy Fitzgerald, whose home village was Horse and Jockey, a tiny hamlet near Cashel, famous for its good racing pub once frequented by Vincent O'Brien and his brother Phonsie. And in the saddle was Mark Dwyer from Finglass. No gymkhana boy he, but a steeplechasing natural who rode Cheltenham as instinctively as if he were competing in a bareback pony race around the housing estates of north Dublin.

Forgive 'N' Forget's potential had originally been spotted by the charismatic Barney Curley, the wily Irish punter who'd also picked out Silver Buck, who won the 1982 Gold Cup for the Dickinson family.

The then six-year-old Forgive 'N' Forget, though only a novice at the time, landed an epic £300,000 gamble at Cheltenham when winning the 1983 Coral Hurdle Final. He was backed down to 5–2 favourite in a field of 23 and turned a supposedly competitive three-mile handicap into a stroll. Such premier league players as J.P. McManus, Michael Tabor, Peter Hopkins and Barney himself had all been part of the plunge and Forgive 'N' Forget and his canny jockey never gave them a moment's worry romping to victory by ten lengths.

'Fitzy' thought he'd timed it to the minute once again when sending Forgive 'N' Forget back to Cheltenham to run in the 1984 SunAlliance Chase for novices. This time Mark Dwyer was injured and John Francome took the ride. He finished second after seeming to leave the chestnut with a lot of ground to make up in the closing stages and riding him wide down the hill. Fitzgerald was incensed. Rumours flew and though Francome has always protested his innocence he never rode for him again.

Dwyer was back for the Gold Cup in '85 and his mount, whose work impressed Peter O'Sullevan, amongst others, on the morning of the race, was given a brilliant ride around the inner. He made ground coming down the hill, flew the last two fences and bounded home by one and a half lengths. He was the best young horse in the field and had been well backed by the 'faces'.

The 1985–86 season had been a quiet one for Forgive 'N' Forget. Malton was hit hard by the ice and snow but things improved just enough to allow the horse to have an away-day gallop at Wetherby racecourse. He did a brilliant piece of work, and with spring on its way Fitzgerald and his staff were convinced that their champion was coming to his peak as usual for the second week of March.

The smart money was in Forgive 'N' Forget's camp but there could be no doubt the classiest chaser in England, at least over three miles, was the great Wayward Lad. The eleven-year-old bay gelding was also trained up in Yorkshire by Mrs Monica Dickinson, mother of Michael, and on Boxing Day 1985 he'd scored his third win in Kempton's Grade One King George VI Chase. Three miles around the flat Sunbury track suited Wayward Lad ideally, as it later suited Desert Orchid, but in a career spanning six seasons he'd yet to win at the Festival and he'd never won over the Gold Cup distance of three and a quarter miles. In the 1983 Gold Cup he'd finished an honourable third to his stable companions Bregawn and Captain John. In 1984 he was sent off favourite but flopped dramatically behind Burrough Hill Lad and in 1985 he flattered turning for home but then faded between the last two fences and finished fifth.

Yet this March, four and a half years after his steeplechasing debut, it seemed the old horse who'd been given a nice rest since Christmas was better than ever. Top-class jumpers had won the Gold Cup at their third or fourth attempt before – Mandarin, The Dikler, Tied Cottage – and with age it seemed that Wayward Lad might also have found extra reserves of stamina. He was a magnificent-looking horse, strong and athletic with a perfect temperament and on his back was the oh-so-talented Graham Bradley, who'd been victorious on Bregawn in 1983. The man they called 'Brad', cavalier and charmer, would end up being warned off for eight years – later reduced to five – in 2002 for his alleged association with the gambler and gangster Brian Wright. But in his prime he was every bit as skilful a horseman as John Francome.

Wayward Lad's trainer Monica Dickinson excelled at training steeplechasers. As redoubtable a character as Jenny Pitman but less inclined to emote or rage for the cameras, she was also running Right Hand Man, who'd been runner-up to Forgive 'N' Forget in 1985. There was Earl's Brig, third in the '85 race; David Elsworth's Combs Ditch, highly rated in the stable and joint favourite for the '83 Gold Cup but more of a Wincanton than a Cheltenham horse; and the Welsh National winner Run And Skip, an ultra-tough stayer who'd also finished second in the 1985 Hennessy Gold Cup.

Peter Easterby, another tough Yorkshireman and a Gold Cup-winning trainer with Alverton and Little Owl, was running Cybrandian, who would go on to be third in the '87 classic. There were two outsiders too: Von Trappe, an ex-handicap hurdler and Festival winner in 1985 and Castle Andrea, 100–1 and running for fun. And then there was number 11 on the racecard. The sole Irish challenger. The eight-year-old bay mare

Dawn Run. Owned by the diminutive 67-year-old Mrs Charmian Hill. Trained at Doninga near Goresbridge in County Kilkenny by the 67-year-old Paddy Mullins. And ridden by the English-based champion jockey and most popular Irishman of them all, the not-quite 34-year-old Jonjo O'Neill.

The mare was set to get a five-pound weight allowance from her rivals, an advantage that had helped her and Jonjo score a famous victory in the Champion Hurdle in 1984. No horse in steeplechasing history had ever gone on from winning the hurdling title – beating fast, ex-flat racing types over two miles – to subsequent triumph in the Gold Cup, the three and a quarter miles with 22 fences staying championship of National Hunt racing.

Could the mare and her never-say-die rider somehow succeed where many others had failed? Could they? Oh, could they indeed? All those discussions – on the radio in Gloucester that Monday morning, with the Irish racegoers in my Oxford hotel, on the way up in the car with David – like countless other conversations in pubs, bars and restaurants throughout Cheltenham and beyond, kept coming back to that one enthralling and overriding question. Could Dawn Run, a daughter of the great jumping stallion Deep Run and one of the most popular and charismatic horses to come out of the Republic since Arkle, really make racing history? Hours and hours of talk and reams of newsprint had already been expended on the issue. What a story it had been and now, with the resolution less than half an hour away, all the arguments raged in my mind once again.

It's not as if the mare hadn't already been at the centre of dramatic and momentous events. The remarkable Mrs Hill, who had hunted all her life, had herself ridden her to victory, at 63 years of age, in a bumper at Tralee in June 1982. When Dawn Run settled into regular training with Paddy Mullins it would be his son Tony who would ride her to 13 of her 21 career wins. But he wasn't in the saddle in March '83 when she finished runner-up in the SunAlliance Hurdle. That day she was ridden by the veteran Gold Cup-winning jockey Ron Barry. And when she won the Champion Hurdle the following season it was Jonjo who took the reins. The County Cork-born rider was the Tony McCoy of his era and his strength, drive and horsemanship, allied to his indomitable will to win, made him the hero of every favourite backer and betting-shop punter in the land.

But Jonjo had something else too, a quality that set him apart from later models like McCoy or Adrian Maguire or Kieran Fallon on the flat. Jonjo had that soft Cork accent and the irresistible smile, albeit one concealing a very shrewd racing brain. You'd be unlikely to see him hurling his whip to the ground as McCoy is prone to do when he falls or fails to ride a winner. Jonjo could be fearsomely hard on a horse but the public had faith in him. Surely with that twinkle and charm he couldn't possibly be hurting them.

John Francome was a greater talent than O'Neill. Francome was a genius. He had flat-racing hands and his ride on Sea Pigeon in the 1981 Champion Hurdle was the most breathtaking display of big-race cool since Lester's Derby on Sir Ivor in 1968. But there were other days when you could sense the punters weren't entirely sure that Francome was doing everything in his power to win. Jonjo, they felt, would never let them down.

Paddy Mullins always said that Dawn Run produced 'a better tune' for his son than for the higher-paid Irishman who rode in England. Jonjo partly refuted that claim when he won the hurdling championship on the mare in '84. She would never have beaten horses like Sea Pigeon and See You Then for speed but against her 1984 rivals she was totally dominant from the moment the tapes went up. The five-pound mare's weight allowance gave her a priceless advantage but it was Jonjo's forcing tactics that drew the sting from her rivals a long way from home. She didn't so much jump the last hurdle as kick it out of the way but by then the race was over.

The celebrations that day were unforgettable but they were only the beginning. There was to be no defence of the hurdling title the following season. Dawn Run went straight over fences, winning a small two-mile race at Navan with ease. Then she suffered an injury, a split pastern, which kept her off the track for a year and would've ended many horses' racing careers right then. Yet there she was, back again in November and December 1985 winning two more novice chases, first at Punchestown then a much more valuable prize at Leopardstown over Christmas. And by the end of that Boxing Day afternoon it was not the King George VI winner Wayward Lad or the champion Forgive 'N' Forget but the mare Dawn Run who was the new favourite for the Cheltenham Gold Cup.

Paddy Mullins had no doubt Dawn Run had both the class and the stamina to bridge the seemingly unbridgeable gap between being the top hurdler and the champion chaser but many bookies and punters in England were scornful of her chances. She was far too inexperienced over the bigger obstacles, they said. Their conviction grew to biblical proportions after her next race. The astute Mullins knew that his horse needed a lesson over English fences. So at the end of January he brought her over to Cheltenham for a serious trial run over three miles and a furlong of the Gold Cup course. Tony Mullins took the ride.

It was a cold but sunny winter's day and a large crowd – part converts, part sceptics – came to watch. Dawn Run looked magnificent and for the first circuit she jumped brilliantly and with such a fluent and commanding stride over the famous turf that I for one was convinced. Yes. Surely. She oozed class. And if she could jump like this in six weeks' time she'd win the big one. Then, just as suddenly, perceptions changed. At the sixth fence from home, on the far side second time around, she got in too close, over-jumped, stumbled on landing and unseated her rider. She was controversially remounted and finished third.

Some felt the incident proved Tony Mullins's fallibility as a jockey. One newspaper rechristened him 'Billy Muggins'. Others felt you couldn't blame the rider for the obviously novicey approach of the horse but Mrs Hill was ruthless. As January faded into February and the snow blanked out racing in England, it emerged that Mullins Junior had been jocked off. That an experienced man had been sent for. And that Jonjo O'Neill would be riding Dawn Run in the Gold Cup.

If Jonjo was alarmed by the scarily limited time he had left to 'get acquainted' with Dawn Run's steeplechasing technique he didn't show it. The odds on a Dawn Run Cheltenham triumph continued to contract as money, especially Irish money, poured onto her. The punters might have been worried if they knew what the 'faces' knew. In late February, O'Neill went over to ride the mare in a schooling session at Gowran Park racecourse and word filtered back to the bookies' offices in England that it had been a disaster, with the Corkman falling off at least once. But there was no question in the owner's mind of calling it off or backing down. There were to be no more prep races either. The icy weather saw to that.

And so here she was. Walking into the paddock at Prestbury Park at 3.15 on the afternoon of 13 March nearly two years to the day since she'd won the Champion Hurdle. Some of the smartest high-rolling bookmakers couldn't see her winning at any price. Victor Chandler laid her to lose well over a quarter of a million and he wasn't the only one to oppose her. Yet it didn't seem to me that any one of her opponents could be backed with confidence either.

Run And Skip, a natural front-runner, was tough and genuine but he was still basically a handicapper. Wayward Lad hadn't stayed three and a quarter miles at Cheltenham before, so why should he do it now? Forgive 'N' Forget was my idea of the real danger. But, thanks again to the weather, he hadn't had a race since Christmas. Admittedly a serious gallop had taken place, purred over by connections, but when he landed over the last fence and hit the uphill finish would a gallop be enough?

Then there was the Jonjo factor. The little man who'd won the 1979 Gold Cup on Alverton, even as sleet and snow swirled over the racecourse. The man who'd waited and waited patiently and then unleashed the great Sea Pigeon to floor the equally iconic Monksfield in their third Champion Hurdle clash in 1980. Jonjo had the rhythm and the strength and he had the confidence.

And then there was the mare. As she walked calmly around the parade ring she seemed to defy you to oppose her. She wasn't pretty. She wasn't a chestnut Oaks-winning filly lusted over by a Derby-winning stallion. She wasn't the classical study of a racehorse at all. But she was big and strong with her rich, bay coat, her long neck and her powerful shoulders and quarters. And she always looked like a winner. She *always* looked a cut above.

With something like the Irish national debt riding on her back, the boards bookmakers were taking no chances. She went off an absurdly short 15–8 favourite but minutes before the off I managed to find a bookie who laid me 2–1. I had on most of what I had in my pockets. A little over £300. No fortune. No fortune to come at those odds either. I knew that many shrewdies and racing professionals would've regarded backing the mare, especially at that price, as an act of sublime folly. But as I have said before there are some betting statisticians who seem to have no soul and no life beyond the *Timeform Black Book*. I was a father for the first time. I was on the high of my life and I'd been waiting years for days like these. Waiting for a horse with the aura, if not the ability, to match Arkle. Unprofessional it may well have been, but I knew that if the mare won and I hadn't backed her I'd never forgive myself. I'd feel that I'd betrayed the spirit of the hour.

Squeezing my way back through the mêlée from the ring and into the Members' Enclosure, I could see the horses parading up the course to my right. Dawn Run – imposing, dominant – was a blur of dark colours. Her bay quarters, the red and black hoops of Charmian O'Neill, Jonjo's black cap. There was Wayward Lad. Calm. Unflappable. Bradley in Mrs Christine Thewliss's maroon jacket with the blue sleeves and the white cap. And there was Forgive 'N' Forget. With Mark Dwyer in Tim Kilroe's bright-yellow jersey with the cherry-red spots. The horse on his toes. His chestnut quarters gleaming. Looking ready and trained to the minute.

I could feel my heart beating faster. I was trying to steel myself for whatever emotion, triumph or despair, would follow. There were many friends amongst the scrum on the lawn but at that moment I felt superstitious about talking and laughing too much. So I stood slightly to one side, keeping my counsel and sinking my hopes in the indefatigable confidence of the Irish section of the crowd.

Down at the start in the pale afternoon light, the runners circled warily. Each jockey focused on his own final preparations. Some talking. One or two of them grim-faced. Jonjo laughing as always. And then the starter called them in.

I looked up briefly from the racecourse and towards the top of Cleeve Hill. Somewhere beyond that ridge was the outside world. Those of us gathered in the sporting congregation – our moods, our faces, mirroring the faces of the jockeys – were lost in our own private world. We would be back in the other place soon enough. Today was for the horses.

CHAPTER TWENTY

Run And Skip, the natural front-runner, was the first away with Dawn Run right there on his outside. Jonjo wasn't going to play any clever-clever games, hanging around the back and dropping the mare out as if she were a flat-racing favourite. It was like Charlie Swan with Like A Butterfly. The ground was good, not testing. O'Neill and Paddy Mullins had absolutely no doubt their horse would stay. Riding her from the front militated against her inexperience, gave her a clear view of the fences and lessened the risk of interference from a stumbling rival. And taking on the field played directly to Dawn Run's strengths and suited her commanding, dominant style.

Throughout the first circuit the mare's jumping was exemplary and as the select band settled down into a rhythm it was Run And Skip and Dawn Run in the front-row seats with Wayward Lad and Forgive 'N' Forget tucked in behind them in around fifth and sixth places, the strong pace seemingly towing the field along like an Olympic distance final. The cards were still all to play.

The punters had cheered Dawn Run on her way down to the start. They cheered her when the race began and they cheered again as the horses swept past the stands and then swung left-handed for the second and final time.

As they raced away into the country with roughly 3 minutes and 20 seconds left, I could feel the hairs standing up on the back of my neck. All the great names in National Hunt history had gone this way before. There could be no private reverie now, though. At the water jump, the second fence down the back straight, Dawn Run made her first mistake. Five fences from home, approaching the top of the hill on the far side, she made another. And this, surely, was the moment when the decision to replace Tony Mullins with J.J. O'Neill was totally vindicated. The Corkman, a natural horseman to the tips of his size 5 boots, sat tight just as Pat Taaffe had done on Arkle 20 years before.

As they reached O'Sullevan's penultimate paragraph and started down the hill, racing deadly seriously now, horses and jockeys straining, waiting and any further mistake likely to prove fatal, Jonjo got the mare balanced again. And so far from playing safe and giving ground he sent her up the inside rail, the shortest but most perilous route. A superb leap three fences from home saw her regain the lead with Run And Skip just beginning to struggle and with only three furlongs and two more obstacles to go.

They came around the final bend and faced up to the second-last fence. Dawn Run took off first and landed in front. Run And Skip couldn't stay with her any longer but here came the others. Wayward Lad, that top-class three-mile chaser so often unlucky at Cheltenham, was closing under a masterful ride from Graham Bradley. And there too on the inside was Forgive 'N' Forget, the handsome chestnut and Festival specialist, cruising under the super-confident Mark Dwyer.

As they raced to the last the Dawn Run story seemed to go into reverse, jubilation turning in a matter of seconds to agonising disappointment tinged with admiration for her game effort. As Wayward Lad came to the fence in front. As Mark Dwyer braced himself for the same kind of race-winning leap on Forgive 'N' Forget, the same kind of momentous propulsion he'd achieved 12 months before. And in their wake Jonjo dropped back into third place, the mare's run seemingly halted, history not to be made.

Over the fence they went but crucially Forgive 'N' Forget wasn't quite so fluent as in 1985. And suddenly it was the 11-year-old Wayward Lad who at last had the Gold Cup in his sights but with that awesome, awful hill still to climb. Halfway up, tiring visibly, he started drifting to his left and there, out of the corner of my eye, I could see the bay mare. The black and red jersey. And Jonjo riding, riding and urging her back up along the stands side rail. Her stamina and courage answering him rhythmically, yes, yes, stride for stride, up they came, the two of them together. The Irish seeing her now too and calling for her en masse, calling from the deepest places. O'Sullevan was calling it unforgettably from his commentary point high up in the stand. 'And the mare's getting up. She's beginning to get up.' And with three lengths to make up from the last and only yards remaining in the race, it was the mare with the black and red hoops who crossed the line first. Wayward Lad finishing a length behind her in second and Forgive 'N' Forget another two and a half lengths back in third.

As Jonjo passed the winning post he punched the air with his fist, his body half-raised in the saddle. It's the image that everyone remembers. The moment of immortality. As his arm went up thousands of Irish punters and racegoers – and many thousands of English, Scottish and Welsh ones too – went up with him, a great wave of emotion lifting every sensate observer off the ground. I was yelling with the best of them. 'She's done it,' I remember shouting at the top of my voice. 'I can't believe it. She's done it.' It had taken 6 minutes and 35 seconds. A course record.

If history had just been made on the track then every racegoer standing down there on the lawn knew instantly that the heroine's return to the winners' circle would also be the scene of a lifetime. And that if they wanted to be there to witness it there was no time to find friends, to talk, to compare impressions or discuss profit and loss. That could come later. So without even waiting to see the horses walk back in front of the stands, I spun on my heel and started running. Racing towards the hopelessly narrow glass doors that funnel spectators from the front of the grandstand to the back.

Thanks to the architectural genius who designed the place, the doors only seemed to open one way and bodies were soon colliding, squashing, smashing, heaving, pressing one into another. Scents of booze, scents of scent, scents of hair oil, sweat and cigar smoke percolating intensely around our foreheads as we all fought to get out, to get through, to battle on from the grandstand to the tiers of terracing overlooking the unsaddling enclosure.

Escaping the crush and haring over the tarmac, I saw and heard a man go down, his bare head hitting the ground with a sickening crunch. Yet in a moment there he was, up on his feet again and running on. By the time Jonjo and Dawn Run entered the paddock at the bottom end, several thousand spectators were packed around the terraces at the top end, and men and women standing at the back were climbing onto walls and shoulders and straining to gaze over heads and hats. Some refused to be corralled and stormed the actual winners' circle itself.

Ten years later the Cheltenham executive introduced safe, sensible and rigorously enforced procedures designed to keep all but the leading players from the unsaddling area. The intention is to cut back on hacks and hangers-on, give the proper connections fair space and priority, give the public an unobstructed view of the horses and protect against the possibility of some intoxicated reveller being felled by a kick to the midriff, balls or skull from an angry and over-excited chaser.

And yet. Deplorable, unacceptable and dangerous it may have been, but what scenes of joyous, riotous mayhem accompanied Dawn Run's return. The whole paddock overrun with delirious Irish punters. Officialdom helpless. The ranks of tweeds and bowlers desperate to maintain protocol but to no avail. Jonjo the hero. Tony Mullins also brought down out of the weighing-room, embraced by the man who'd deposed him and lifted shoulder high. Dawn Run still snorting, her powerful flanks heaving from her exertions, stamping her foot, her big neck and head cradled by Mrs Hill and her son Ollie.

Irish racegoers launching into song. The sound of 'Here We Go, Here We Go, Here We Go' sending tangible shivers of alarm through some of the better-bred tweeds. Toffs present thinking they were hearing the revolutionary battle cry of Arthur Scargill's troops from the recent miners' strike. But this was a benign anthem, more a chorus of Barry McGuigan supporters than a flashback to the Battle of Orgreave. Even so a team of Jockey Club Stewards, led by Lieutenant Colonel Sir Piers Bengough, could be seen mounting an inadvisably small podium and stiffening every moustachioed upper lip and blue-blooded sinew in an attempt to restore discipline. One of them whacking at bodies ineffectually with a rolled-up umbrella. A bowler suddenly flying through the air like a decapitated head at the start of a Shakespearean riot. The despairing Sir Piers and his men increasingly taking on the stance of upstanding chaps fighting to keep back the colonial hordes. Saving their penultimate bullet for the memsahib and another for themselves.

The hysterical attempts to keep order were as unsuccessful as they were fundamentally unnecessary. The Queen Mother, to her eternal credit, showed no alarm or displeasure at all as she was ushered totteringly, smilingly, through the crowd to present the precious Cup to Mrs Hill and the accompanying prizes to Paddy Mullins and then to Jonjo. And though many Irishmen may still insist that Tony Mullins 'got on' with the mare best of all, they had O'Neill to thank in their prayers that night for the bets landed, the pounds and punts won and the stories to tell their grandchildren.

They'd waited six years since the last Irish-trained Gold Cup winner, Tied Cottage, and he was subsequently disqualified on a technicality. They'd waited 14 years since L'Escargot and 20 since Arkle. Now at last the sport had another record-breaking Irish champion to join the pantheon of the greats. And while Cheltenham in March may nowadays appeal, brilliantly and successfully, to a great swathe of new racegoers, as much from the towns and cities as the rural shires, it remains fundamentally in spirit and atmosphere an Irish rather than an English occasion. They've made it what it is. From Vincent O'Brien to Tom Dreaper and Dan Moore. And from Mick O'Toole and Eddie O'Grady to Willie Mullins, Aidan O'Brien and Charlie Swan. They've brought the horses and the jockeys, the owners, the breeders and the punters. They've brought the skill, the cunning and the humour. And most of all they've brought the passion and taught the rest of us exactly what it means.

The joy of racing, the joy of all sport, is that there are always new names to look out for and new contests to excite, so there can be no place for gloomy reflections that the magic of the old days can never be regained. Yet in some respects Dawn Run's Gold Cup was a high watermark in the evolution of Cheltenham. It was the climax of a golden era that began with the fabulous Champion Hurdle battles between Night Nurse, Monksfield and Sea Pigeon in the mid-'70s and enjoyed an encore with Desert Orchid's emotional Gold Cup victory in 1989.

It was a time when the racing and the party still felt as if it was being staged predominantly for the truly knowledgeable devotees. A time when corporate entertaining was still in its infancy and pink-faced chaps from Allied Dunbar and Invesco Trust, clutching badges for a hospitality package in Chalet 129E, were less likely to get in the way and make a nuisance of themselves than they are now. It was a time before the compulsory purchase of tickets in advance. A time before the bars were shut half an hour after the last. A time when the celebrations on course went on until well after dark.

It was a time before all those short cuts through the surrounding countryside had been discovered. A time before all the best pubs were oversubscribed. A time before excessive media analysis and pontification and pomposity. A time before relentless brand identification and fatuous marketing campaigns. A time before the British Horseracing Board and its intemperate chairman Peter Savill. A time too before an unholy alliance of the BHB and the big off-course bookmaking chains combined to introduce a new tax on on-course bookies that threatens to drive many of them out of business altogether, tilting starting prices further in favour of the big combines and destroying the betting-ring atmosphere that makes a British racecourse unique.

It was a time before face-painting and bouncy castles and Sunday family fun days. A time before a minor soap star and some refugee from daytime TV were regarded as essential aids to sell the sport of racing to the public. A time when the passion, drama and spectacle of horses racing and the adrenalin thrill of gambling on them was the undiminished essence of the story.

There were four other contests that afternoon but I remember little of them. The rest of the day was given over to tumultuous and all-consuming inebriation. And the best place to be was in the Arkle Bar down towards the bottom of the lawn by the walkway through to the paddock and the Old Toffs' boxes.

The Arkle Bar, as it was then, was very different to the modernised, concrete version that replaced it in 1990. The new bar has framed newspaper cuttings of Himself and Pat Taaffe on the wall but unfortunately that's where the atmosphere begins and ends. The new bar is cramped and angular with unwelcoming brown doors and a small, brick patio. The old bar was a great barn of a place. Bare and high-ceilinged with wooden floors and a paraffin-burning stove in the centre. It was a place to eat oysters and drink champagne and Guinness. A place to order brandy, sloe gin and whisky mac. There were wooden ledges to rest the drinks on and a long, wooden, formica-topped bar, behind which, legend has it, Tommy Carberry enjoyed a few hours' sleep after passing out and being accidentally locked in the night before he won his first Gold Cup on L'Escargot in 1970.

In 1987 this was the scene of frontier saloon-style wildness, as snow fell on the course delaying the start of the Gold Cup and two Irish girls danced and stripped on the table tops. Security men sent to calm things down – and no doubt keen to see the show – were kept out by the punters.

That March afternoon in '86 the Arkle Bar was similarly packed and rocking and standing in the centre of the room was one of the most charismatic of all Irish racing characters. Aidan

'Suntan' O'Connell. Tall and darkly handsome. Gambler, charmer, chancer and con-man. A sometime horse dealer. A fine rider to hounds in County Limerick. A man in a long coat who wore his hair in a pony tail years before it became a common fashion statement. A serial seducer. A man with an accountancy degree from a South African university. A man who once took a bet that he could ride in the Grand National and survive a circuit. And who then took a room in the Savoy, training hard, naturally, by running up the embankment each morning and then returning to be greeted by a hotel porter with a stopwatch in one hand and a Bloody Mary in the other. Unfortunately when he got to Aintree he fell off at Becher's first time round.

This same Irishman has at various points been warned off all British racecourses for 'irregularities' of one kind or another. March 1986 coincided with one of those periods of exclusion but no security man or representative of the law – or the Jockey Club or the racecourse manager – was likely to get their hands on him that day. And even if they had, an adoring Irish entourage, male and female, would have made his eviction difficult, not to say impossible.

And who would've wanted to evict him anyway or given a damn at that moment about assorted incidents on file? O'Connell, like many of racing's repeat offenders, was the most charmingly roguish of men and irresistibly good company. As we all gathered round him that March afternoon, he stood impressively tall and smiling, leading chorus after chorus of 'The Wild Rover', 'Kevin Barry' and 'The Fields Of Athenry'. Along with a special tribute to Dawn Run. 'She's got the Gold Cup in her hands, she's got the Gold Cup in her hands . . . '

There were so many flushed and excited faces, British as well as Irish. David Tupman was there and so too was another great friend – and charmer and chancer – the writer and journalist Simon Bell, who had made contact with Suntan for the purposes of magazine research in Ireland the previous month.

As darkness fell outside, the songs and the drink kept flowing and the adrenalin-charged intensity of the Festival continued to rage like an uncontrollable forest fire. All the racecourse lights were on now and burning brightly. Empty bottle after empty bottle piled high into the crates behind the stand. The betting-ring floor awash with litter and discarded betting slips and abandoned pages of form. The phosphorescent whiteness of the running rail glowing in the dark. And the helicopters flying overhead – like Vietnam behind the lines, joked somebody – as we stumbled out into the car park, somehow finding David's motor in the dim recesses of the field and negotiating the half-mile to the De La Bere Hotel at Southam, where O'Connell's party reassembled.

In the hot, packed and noisy hotel bar, Aidan stood with his back to a wooden beam. He had a smile on him like a fox in a chicken-run. On one side was an extremely attractive Irish woman aged, I would guess, in her late 40s. On the other side was the self-same Irish woman's extremely attractive daughter aged, perhaps, 21 or 22. Each woman had her eyes on Aidan while Simon Bell optimistically had his eyes on the daughter. He had placed his right hand on the wooden beam above her head and was tentatively sliding it down towards her back. But in Suntan he was taking on a womaniser of the highest calibre.

As the drink got to Simon his arm kept sliding off the beam, his legs sagging. O'Connell meanwhile, displaying an epic capacity for alcohol, drew the mother in effortlessly with one arm and the daughter with the other. They were both glowing with excitement.

Up at the other end of the room the hail-fellow husband and father – red-faced, intoxicated and busy buying drinks all round – never saw it happening and was almost certainly past doing anything about it anyway. As Tupman and I returned from a trip to buy cigars at the bar, we suddenly realised that Aidan and the ladies had gone. Departed, all three of them, upstairs to O'Connell's room for a no doubt much-needed 'rest' before dinner.

More bottles were ordered but Bell needed reviving and we all needed food. With company to entertain there seemed little prospect of Suntan rejoining us any time soon but David, Simon and I were determined to finish the day, and the week, in style with a celebratory meal. Tupman had loyally booked us into one of his favourite restaurants, the Rose Tree in Bourton, but as he pulled out of the De La Bere car park and started back up Cleeve Hill, it was overwhelmingly apparent that he was not only far too drunk to drive but was indeed so far gone that he would be unable to take any further part in the proceedings. And three minutes up the road he sensibly swung off to the right into the car park of the Rising Sun Hotel. David got out. Simon and I got out. And then David climbed into the back seat, locked the doors and passed out.

Not really thinking at that moment about precisely how we were going to get home or back to Oxford or London or wherever, Simon and I decided we must still have dinner come what may. I myself was hungry and excited enough to eat for three.

We walked down the hill to the Malvern View Hotel, which in those days had a *Good Food Guide* listed restaurant, and by a piece of spectacular good luck it transpired they'd just that second had a cancellation. Excellent. There was a log fire burning in the bar and Bell and I ordered regally. There would be lobster and rare roast beef. There would be wines of pedigree and expense. I still had over a monkey (£500) from the afternoon's racing so there was no question of not going for it.

I got up to go to the Gents', leaving Simon cradling a large Bloody Mary. When I returned I found him passed out on the sofa. After much persuasion he came to but not soberly enough to satisfy the restaurant manager, who suddenly remembered the other party hadn't cancelled after all or, more likely, he'd just decided our presence wasn't the asset he'd imagined.

Seeing the prospect of dinner snatched away from me like some cartoon cat who never quite gets his paws on the pizza, I reluctantly accepted the manager's edict. I didn't much fancy eating a three-course meal on my own anyway – the only solitary diner in the Cotswolds that night – but perhaps fresh air would make Simon recover and we could go somewhere else. Initially it did the trick as, with one final burst of energy, we surged back up the hill to the Rising Sun. David was still insensible in the back seat of his car but Bell and I rolled on into the brightly lit hotel – not Michelin or *Good Food Guide* standard maybe, but serving hot food nonetheless. Steak and chips. A few bottles of wine. Some apple pie and ice cream. We should've been so lucky. The Rising Sun restaurant was packed to overflowing and in that era, with the clock moving on towards 10.30 p.m., the dreaded announcement, 'The kitchen closes in ten minutes' time', didn't bode well.

A less-than-beaming functionary declared that they 'might be able to run up a sandwich', at which point Simon passed out for the third and final time, sitting on a chair in the foyer. 'You can't leave him there,' declared the functionary. 'We'll have to put him outside in the car park.'

The thought of Bell being dumped on the ground was too dreadful to contemplate but even if he hadn't been comatose I couldn't arrange for him to share the warm and fetid closeness of David's car because Tupman had locked himself in with the keys. Then I discovered that some of the Rising Sun's Festival guests, no doubt brimful of their joyous hospitality, had already checked out and a bed was available. Simon's details were taken and two porters dragged him off down a corridor, a hand under each arm. His exit resembled that of a slain bull being towed from the ring.

What we didn't realise at the time – I was drunk too, don't forget – was that Simon's Access card had no credit on it and he had next to no cash left either. So Friday morning began with him waking up, fully dressed, in a strange hotel room with absolutely no idea how he got there and no ability to pay for it. Sensibly he made his escape through the bedroom window and across a flower bed, eventually hitching a lift into Cheltenham where he found someone to cash him an IOU enabling him to take a train back to London.

That was Friday. Late on Thursday night, finding myself alone, I suddenly knew I didn't want to stay in the Rising Sun. I wanted to go back to Oxford. Not to the John Radcliffe maybe.

Not in my drunken state and not at that time of night, but back to the Linton Lodge to at least be spiritually closer to Emma and Jack, the easier and quicker to see them the following day. So I had a Guinness and a beef sandwich sitting in the hotel foyer, raising my glass one last time to Jonjo and Dawn Run, to Tupman, Bell and O'Connell. And then I spent a chunk of the cash I'd won on a 1 a.m. cab ride back to Oxford.

It was a strangely muted and solitary end to the week. But you never forget the intensity of those feelings. They've stayed with me, year on year, sharpened and refined every March, a constant spur in the quest for an even better horse and for an even bigger and better Festival experience to top the last one.

That particular fiesta, though, was over. And I was about to experience the fleeting and ephemeral nature of all such moments of exultation and joy. As I should've remembered from my first Cheltenham 25 years before, the post-Festival come-down is the most brutal of them all.

CHAPTER TWENTY-ONE

I was sitting in my mother-in-law Susie Vereker's car and we were driving along the lower road from Cirencester to Cheltenham. It was Thursday, 3 April. Exactly three weeks to the day since Dawn Run had won the Gold Cup. There was no sunshine this morning either but it was greyer and colder than March with a chill breeze.

This was also the opening day of the Grand National meeting up at Aintree and I was meant to be there. Not just to socialise either but to do some work for a magazine. I was beginning to understand the truth of another of Jeffrey Bernard's comments about 'skating on thin ice', not being a sport you could fully comprehend until you started writing about racing professionally. Emma, Jack and I had gone over from Naunton to Fairford the previous evening so that they would be safe in the arms of the family until I returned from Liverpool on the Saturday night.

Shortly after getting up on Thursday morning Susie called me downstairs. There was a telephone call from a GP in Bourton-on-the-Water, where my parents had moved to six months before. My father had suffered a heart attack and been rushed to Cheltenham General Hospital. My mother had gone with him in the ambulance and would meet me there.

This wasn't Larkin's first coronary coming like Christmas. That had come eight years before, arriving in October 1978, three years after I left Oxford. I seem destined to associate the most dramatic moments of my life with race meetings and that first big attack was on a Sunday, the day Lester Piggott won the Prix de l'Arc De Triomphe for the second year running on the great Alleged, who was trained by Vincent O'Brien. I caught snatches of O'Sullevan's commentary on a ward TV in the Kent and Sussex Hospital in Tunbridge Wells, much as I'd watched High Top and Roberto in the 2,000 Guineas in 1972.

That first coronary truly had a sense of inevitability about it. My father's father had died of heart disease. And his grandfather. And two uncles. And his brother George. It was a congenital family weakness. Add to that Alex's life-long fondness for tobacco. When I was a child he smoked Players Navy Cut, later switching to a pipe, and the silver cigarette box in our house was always full. Add to that the years of mounting stress and overwork at Chiesmans and the accompanying angina and, in retrospect, an appointment with disaster was unavoidable.

Once it became clear that he'd survived and that he wasn't going to die, not then, I remember the look of exhaustion on his face. Sitting up in his hospital bed, he wasn't just grateful to be alive he was visibly relieved that the trauma anticipated for so long had finally happened. It wasn't a stroke. His brain wasn't damaged. And the prognosis wasn't that bad. Maybe he'd make it.

It did for his working life, though, and on medical advice he retired in January 1979, leaving a year earlier than expected. On his final day at Chiesmans they gave him a party in the old top-floor restaurant. All the staff came, everyone signing his card from the general manager to the chefs in the kitchen. The scene was caught on camera by a photographer for the *Kent and Sussex Courier*. Looking at the picture now it seems like a snapshot from a vanished era. Everyone gathered round like the cast of *Are You Being Served?* Alex smiling shyly. And a Mr Rumbold character shaking hands and presenting him with his farewell envelope.

My father loved retirement. It was a blissful release from the years of drudgery and he and my mother couldn't have been happier together. My mother's great fear, though, was of them growing old alone in Tunbridge Wells, especially after Margaret Butcher died of cancer in 1983. That's how they came to move from Kent to Gloucestershire.

When I heard about the second heart attack my immediate reaction was, 'Oh no. Not now. Just give them a few more good years together to enjoy a new home, a new place. Even two or three would be something.' I said this to Susie Vereker in the car. 'I don't think there's ever a good time for one of your parents to die,' she said wisely.

It felt very strange to be walking back into a hospital emergency unit less than a month after Jack's birth. Cheltenham General – improved, brightened and modernised in recent years – felt old and gloomy with dark corridors and a shabby decor more 1956 than '86. In the small, intensive-care ward the beds were squeezed in side by side in the old-fashioned manner with an aisle between. The walls were painted a cheerless yellow and there was blue lino on the floor. Only a window facing out onto the College Ground, site of the annual county cricket festival in July, lightened the atmosphere.

My mother was waiting in a room at the end of the ward. She hadn't seen Alex since he'd been brought in. A doctor took us to one side and explained that my father was holding on but that the next 36 hours would be crucial. He added that we might be shocked by his appearance when we saw him. A coronary of that severity ravaged the face and body and we would see a lot of tubes and monitoring machines but we should not be frightened by them. They were normal and necessary in the circumstances.

When I did see my father in bed I understood why the doctor had been so considerate. Alex, who'd looked spruce and well on his 70th birthday only 15 months before, seemed to have aged 10 years overnight. His head was tilted back, his hair ruffled, his mouth half-open and his complexion a deathly grey. He was on a drip and there was a tube up his nose and heart monitors on his chest. His hospital pyjama jacket was unbuttoned and you could almost see where the heart's convulsions had left a mark across his torso like an earthquake's fault line or the trail of an electric current. A life-support machine, so beloved by TV medical dramas, bleeped away by the bed.

He was drifting in and out of consciousness but when we sat down quietly beside him he opened his eyes. 'Why aren't you at Aintree?' he asked me. He couldn't say much more and the sister didn't want him to talk for long anyway. They'd given him morphine to counteract the pain and it made him intermittently sick. We just sat there for as long as we were allowed and held his hand. Later that morning the same doctor explained that he'd been diagnosed with left-sided heart failure. We nodded as if in knowledgeable comprehension of every detail.

We came and went throughout that day and evening. I could feel myself slipping into the same kind of automatic survival mode that had descended in the sitting-out room on the labour ward at the John Radcliffe. As long as I kept talking and didn't allow doubts and fears to grow in the silences, it seemed possible to convince myself and my mother that the worst needn't happen.

In the town and the countryside all around us spring was full on. The blooming, flowering scent of it. In the air and on the shrubs and trees. Everything starting again. New and infinitely detailed like a baby's DNA. In the face of such evidence of creation, I said, of providence, of life after death, how could we possibly imagine anything other than a full recovery for Alex? He'd got over it six years before. He'd get over it again. I don't know whether my mother really believed anything I was saying. I'm not sure if I believed it myself but, as Ernest Hemingway once wrote, 'No horse called Morbid ever won a race.'

And over the following days Alex first rallied and then seemed to come back to life in front of our eyes. There was a morning when I was able to spend over an hour with him, the two of us chatting together in low voices. His jacket was done up this time, his hair had been washed and brushed and he was well enough to smile at the ever-present nurses who'd taken a protective shine to him and smiled back.

One afternoon Emma and I went in to visit him and took Jack with us. My father was sitting up in bed and we put the baby in his arms. He'd seen his latest grandson several times already, of course. Jack sat there contentedly, making a few gurgling noises but otherwise quite peaceful, perhaps touched by his grandfather's calm as I had always been. The baby was all washed and clean and bright-eyed and my father stroked his head very gently and breathed in his fresh and still newly born smell. And I honestly believe that something inside him, acknowledging a new generation, felt that it was going to be all right, that he'd done enough and that whatever happened to him the family would go on.

The following week he went home, travelling once again with my mother in an ambulance. She remembers him feasting his eyes on the primroses and cherry blossom along the way. 'He seemed so glad to be alive,' she said.

On Saturday, 19 April we went over to visit them. Jack was asleep this time. The food in the hospital had been revolting and my father joked about the many delicious things he'd like to eat and the simpler things the doctors had told him to eat. He had my mother to tease and cherish. She had him to love and look after. They were both happy and smiling as they waved goodbye.

Around four o' clock on Sunday morning I woke up and saw Emma standing at the foot of the bed in her dressing-gown. She held my gaze steadily and I knew what she was going to say. The doctor in Bourton had just rung, she explained. 'Your father has had another heart attack . . . and this time he's died.'

I felt a tightening around my chest and head, so tight that I could hardly breathe. And as I got out of bed and started to get dressed my legs went numb. I called a taxi and rode down to Bourton just as daylight was breaking. 'I'll remember these things,' I thought. 'The silent taxi. The empty road. The reddening sky. I'll remember them all my life.'

When I got to my parents' house, the lights on unnaturally early, the local doctor greeted me at the door. He seemed genuinely upset. My mother was sitting on the sofa in her dressing-gown, the family dog, a Jack Russell, looking on confused and silent. She had a photograph of my father in her hands and the tears were running down her face. I sat down next to her and we put our arms around each other.

She told me that in the ambulance on the way into Cheltenham that morning three weeks before, Alex, though in excruciating pain, had gripped her arm and said, 'You've been the light of my life for over forty-five years.' Forty-five years. More than four decades. One marriage. One lover. One constant companion. In good times and bad. For richer and poorer. In stoicism and joy. It's almost impossible to imagine a relationship like that in the early twenty-first century. Yet the longer it lasted, the more terrible the loneliness was going to be for the one who was eventually left behind.

I felt an imperative need to be strong, to hold things together, to see it through. What is it? A very English reaction, I suppose. Something we were brought up with in the post-war era. Well, I tried my best but when I went upstairs to my parents' bedroom the façade cracked.

It's hard to find the words that can adequately describe the experience of staring down at your father's dead body. He was lying on his side in the bed in his pyjamas. My mother said that he'd woken in the night and taken a sip of water. Then he lay down again and a few minutes later she heard a long sigh. She believed that he'd died in his sleep and felt no pain. I wanted to believe the same.

Just over a month before I'd watched my first child coming into the world. Now I had a shattering reminder of his and my own mortality. The fledgling story barely begun. Yet one day it would end like this – unless, God forbid, I outlive my children – with them looking down too, losing a father or mother as I had just done.

I looked at Alex's grey hair and moustache, at the wedding ring on his finger and at his strong arms. His eyes were still open. I leaned across to close them and suddenly realised, in a banal but terrifying way, just how over and finite death really is. I could talk, I could cry, I could scream and rage but my father couldn't hear me. No matter what I did, he couldn't respond. Where there had been smiles, laughter, breath, a heartbeat, a pulse, there was nothing. Just a lifeless form. Heavy and grey. The body's heat already cooling. The soul already gone . . . who knows where?

I kissed him gently on the forehead. I could feel the emotion coming from a long way back like an onrushing and unstoppable tide. And for several minutes I just knelt down beside him on the floor and cried and cried. Images of childhood flashed through my mind. The excitement of his early return from work on Christmas Eve. The feeling that it couldn't properly begin until he was there. The joy of being in his company for two whole weeks in the summer holiday. Always an early riser, he would often come into my room and suggest that we went for a walk along the beach before breakfast. The newly washed sand. Yachts at anchor. A mackerel fisherman heading out to sea. And the two of us exploring rock pools and scanning the horizon for signs of ships. A tanker maybe or a ferry or an ocean liner. The *Queen Mary* or the *United States*. Returning to Southampton from New York.

Together. Close. Happy. The feel of his clothes. His smell. His smile. Always dependable. Always there. How could I possibly manage without him?

As the long day began there was a list of people to ring up. My sister and brother. Old family friends. And men who'd known my father and worked with him in the Tunbridge Wells years and before. And of course there was also the undertaker. Mr Wright. A memorably Hardyesque figure. Death personified. Walking up to my mother's front door in his black suit and tie. His concern impeccably professional. His ample presence designed to reassure.

Mr Wright and his assistant took away my father's body. They wrapped him up in a sheet and as they carried him downstairs they made me think of Alex himself hauling rolls of carpet into the Chiesmans window years before.

That night I had a dream that I was in my mother's back

garden when the gate opened and in walked my father. He was in a jacket and trousers and an open-necked shirt. He explained that he hadn't died after all and that it had all been a terrible mistake. He was smiling and relieved and was just about to tell me what had happened when I woke up. I've had that dream many times since.

The funeral was on the Friday. A brilliant spring day. My mother, my sister, my brother and I all made an effort to protect ourselves by dressing smartly, though not too sombrely, dark glasses at the ready, as if with such little sartorial gestures you can somehow keep grief at bay. Of course you can't. I'd felt no desire to see my father, rouged and brushed up, in Mr Wright's chapel of rest in Stow. I preferred to remember him as he was, but my mother and I liked the idea of his coffin being brought to the church the night before the service. It seemed a homely touch. I'd forgotten that nothing can prepare you for the shock of walking in and being confronted by the overwhelming finality of a wooden box.

Setting out from the house for the church again the following day, I felt as if I were moving in slow motion. Legs numb, head and chest stretched tight. We got through the hymns, the readings, the favourite piece of poetry, the vicar's address. They were all fine and moving. The last part was the worst. First the onward journey to the crematorium half-an-hour's drive away. The modern, efficient and thoroughly Ortonesque terminus of Alex Reid's life. Turning up the drive, we saw daffodils and tastefully landscaped conifers concealing, but not entirely, the tastefully discreet chimney. There was the usual queue of mourners waiting for their loved ones to be despatched at 20-minute intervals. It was all very organised. The timetable was on the wall in the foyer for all to see. A. Reid. 3.30 p.m.

Inside the wretchedly varnished chapel the electronic organ played. The undertakers arranged the coffin for the final time and then stood respectfully to one side. Mr Wright, in his black frock coat, looking like a Royal Ascot punter who's done his pieces on the last. The vicar spoke the words and then, right on schedule, an unseen button was pressed, the curtains opened and the coffin started to recede. My mother sobbed, the curtains closed and I felt as if I were going over Niagara Falls in a barrel.

The drive back through the sunlit countryside would've been glorious at any other time. There was still tea to be got through with relations in a country hotel then later that evening my sister and I took my mother to the pub. It was barely six weeks since the Cheltenham Gold Cup. Forty-six days since Jack was born. And the year's quota of drama was not over yet.

On 26 June my oldest and closest friend, and the love of my life at university a dozen years before, died of cancer. She was 32 years old and she had an 18-month-old baby. And then in November, at the year's end, dear old Gilbert Butcher, confused and rambling without Margaret, died of a heart attack in Chiddingstone. It was my third funeral in seven months. A birth and three funerals. I couldn't have taken any more. Even the racing stories seemed to have borrowed their cue from the sequence of sadness and personal loss.

On 30 April 1986 the Punchestown Festival – Ireland's greatest steeplechase meeting which takes place on the edges of Naas in County Kildare – staged a special one-off match race between Dawn Run and the two-mile champion chaser Buck House. Vincent O'Brien himself suggested it and Coolmore Stud put up part of the IR£25,000 purse, with Seamus Purcell and Punchestown racecourse also contributing shares.

The distance and the conditions, two and a quarter miles on good fast ground, should've been ideal for Buck House and they bet 11–8 Tommy Carmody's mount and 4–6 the mare. Dawn Run was supposed to have stamina in excess of speed and Tony Mullins, who'd replaced Jonjo, knew that he had to make the running and try to stretch his rival long before the end. Coming to the last Buck House challenged her, all guns blazing, but he couldn't get by. Mullins remembers the mare literally gritting her teeth in defiance. She came home two and a half lengths clear and her return to unsaddle was accompanied by more unprecedented scenes of tumultuous celebration.

That brief spring and early summer Dawn Run was the most famous and revered sporting figure in all Ireland, north and south, and her achievements made her the biggest racing story since Red Rum. Almost everyone now wanted her to be given a rest over the summer so that she could be brought back again, fit and well, to defend her Gold Cup crown the following season. Mrs Hill had other ideas. She wanted to run her horse in the French Champion Hurdle or Grande Course de Haies at Auteuil on 27 June. Dawn Run had taken the three-mile prize two years before and still appeared comfortably superior to even the best French hurdlers. The race was worth 500,000 French francs, roughly equivalent to £41,000 sterling, a lavish jumping prize at the time and some said Mrs Hill needed the money.

It was a dry and sunny day in Paris. The going was firm. And the French jockey Michel Chirol, not Tony Mullins, not Jonjo, was in the saddle. With over a mile still to run, Dawn Run was challenging for the lead when she took off too soon at the eighth flight of hurdles, and fell heavily, breaking her neck. She died instantly.

All sections of the racing community were stunned by what had happened. Any racehorse, and not just a chaser or hurdler, can die any day of the week, be it at Cheltenham or Redcar or just stumbling on the gallops one morning. It's an unavoidable aspect of the sport and over and over again I've tried to convince myself that if you can't deal with that fact you shouldn't get involved. But it doesn't make the losses any easier to cope with. The mare was still only eight years old. She'd run 35 times, winning 21 races and over £340,000 worth of prize money. The pleasure and excitement she gave to those of us who followed her on the track is impossible to put a price on.

A few years later I went over to Ireland in February for a week's racing and 'research' in the lead-up to another National Hunt Festival. There was a big Saturday meeting at Punchestown, a point-to-point at Fairyhouse on the Sunday and the following Wednesday an interesting but more low-key gathering back at Leopardstown, six miles south of Dublin city centre.

When I got to the Foxrock track that day I went in through the main door of the stand and walked up to the Hall of Fame on the first floor. There were Arkle's famous colours in the display case straight ahead of me. The Duchess's yellow jersey with the black hoop and the black cap. And there in a case alongside were another set of racing colours. The black and red jacket worn by Jonjo on Dawn Run surrounded by other photographs, letters and memorabilia. The mare's life and career commemorated alongside Arkle himself. The only horse deemed fit to share his space. The two of them together, side by side now and forever. It had been almost 20 years exactly from Arkle's third Gold Cup to Dawn Run's day of days, 13 March 1986. Twenty years. And that's the story.

After my father's death, and after the death of Dawn Run, I found it hard to make sense of things. Seventeen years later I would say that racing, especially racing at Cheltenham, has given me the best and most memorable days of my life or been inextricably linked with them and with the people who have illuminated them. So Arkle and Mill House are forever associated with my grandmother Mrs Tanner. And Lester and Sir Ivor, Nijinsky and Roberto mean growing up and escaping from the Judd School and from Tonbridge and Tunbridge Wells. And Dawn Run and that epic 1986 Gold Cup will forever be associated with the elation of my son's birth and the pain and loss of my father's death. And returning to Cheltenham, year after year, is a way of celebrating those people who gave me life and who encouraged me to appreciate all of these things in the first place.

There have been other winners since 1986. And I have seen other great champions, both over the jumps and on the flat, from Epsom to Longchamp and Churchill Downs. There have been losers too. And debts, disasters and insolvency hearings. But that's another story.

There are some punters for whom racing is just a cover for the addictive and neurasthenic intensity of gambling itself, be it on horses, dogs or two flies crawling up a wall. I know people like that. They enthral me but I'm not one of them. For myself and for others like me the attraction is not just the wager but the whole human and equine story behind it. The character, personality and passion. Allied to the sheer and indefatigable belief that in racing – and maybe in life too – no matter what befalls, there's always another day. It's a faith not lightly held and sometimes clung to in the face of pain, reversal and intense despair . . . but it's clung to nonetheless.

POSTSCRIPT

Cheltenham racecourse. Six p.m, 13 March 2003. Another year. Another Festival over. Twenty races. And fourteen winning favourites. Glory for the punters. Catastrophe for the layers. 'It's been a blood bath,' says Freddie Williams as he and his colleagues hobble out of the ring like a column of departing refugees.

The trading floor coated with rubbish. Newsprint. Racecards. Losing betting slips. Urinals choked with fag ends. The fast-food stalls packing up but the air still tinged with fumes. Hot dogs and burgers. Hot 'pork' and chicken. Fish and fries and sugared doughnuts.

Highlights of the day's racing replaying on the big screen. And the helicopters flying out, the sound echoing mournfully over the emptying racecourse. As squadrons of police move in to clear the bars. Sweeping out the drunks and the stragglers like the refuse collectors clattering bin after binload of junk into their lorries.

Like A Butterfly, my heroine of 2002, didn't win the Champion Hurdle, for which I'd backed her ante-post at 16–1. She didn't even show. Rhinestone Cowboy didn't win it either. He was beaten once again but not embarrassed. An honourable third. Not another Sea Pigeon perhaps, not yet, but the dream lives on.

In the very first race of the meeting though, the Supreme Novices Hurdle of 2003, we hit them right between the eyes. Back In Front. Third in the Bumper 12 months before. Twice a winner in Ireland in the winter of 2002/3. And trained by Eddie O'Grady. A Cheltenham specialist nonpareil. 'He would be right up there with the best of the novices I've sent to the meeting down the years,' he'd confided two weeks before.

I'd already backed the horse at 10–1 in December. A hundred each way. At 7–1 in January. At 7–2 in March. They sent him off the 3–1 favourite. And there he was in the spring sunshine. Cruising down the hill with 'Storming' Norman Williamson oozing confidence. The sight you wait all year to see. The Irish banker. Pulling double, two out, in the opener at Cheltenham. And there's no Pizarro to worry about this time. No Adamant Approach either, or Westender. There's no danger. And I hear myself talking out loud standing down there on the lawn, jammed in with all the others. 'Go on, Norman. He's running away. He's running away . . .'

Why do we do it? We do it because it's like falling in love. And as long as the joy exceeds, even marginally, the inevitable and unavoidable pain . . . I'll never stop. Never.